OVER THE MOUNTAINS AND THE SEA

First edition: 2023
© publication: Gwasg Carreg Gwalch
© text: the authors
© illustrations: Elin Manon

All rights reserved. No part of this publication may be reproduced, stored in a retrieval system, or transmitted in any form or by any means, electronic, electrostatic magnetic tape, mechanical, photocopying, recording or otherwise, without the prior permission of the publisher, Gwasg Carreg Gwalch, 12 Iard yr Orsaf, Llanrwst, Dyffryn Conwy, Cymru LL26 0EH.

ISBN: 978-1-84527-935-6

Published with the financial support of the Books Council of Wales
Illustrator: Elin Manon
Designer: Olwen Fowler
Translation: Jane Burnard

 Published by Gwasg Carreg Gwalch,
12 Iard yr Orsaf, Llanrwst, Dyffryn Conwy, Cymru LL26 0EH.
Tel: 01492 642031
www.carreg-gwalch.cymru

Printed and published in Wales

OVER THE MOUNTAINS AND THE SEA

Tales of Brave Celtic Women

Translated by Jane Burnard

Contents

page	
8	Golden-headed Niamh (Ireland)
14	Rhiannon and the Punishment of Being a Horse (Wales)
20	Ker Is (Brittany)
26	Morag the Clever (Scotland)
32	The Giants of Karrek Loos yn Koos (Cornwall)
38	The Mermaid of Purt le Moirrey (Isle of Man)
44	An Eye for an Eye and a Tooth for a Tooth (Ireland)
50	Rhos y Pawl (Wales)
56	The Daughter of the Waves (Scotland)
62	The Adventure of Keresen of Sen Senar (Cornwall)
68	The Story of Gráinne (Ireland)
74	Azenor, the Wise and Beautiful (Brittany)
80	Pennard Castle (Wales)
86	Cailleach – Keeper of the Deer (Scotland)
92	Queen Lupa of Galicia (Galicia)

These legends were chosen and adapted into Welsh by:
Angharad Tomos, Haf Llewelyn, Mari George,
Aneirin Karadog, Myrddin ap Dafydd,
Anni Llŷn and Branwen Williams

Keeping stories alive

Celts have settled in the rocky landscapes on the edges of western Europe. In the places where beautiful, hidden sea shores and coves full of secrets lie. Where the forms of giants are found in rocks and the whispers of the fair folk overheard in caves. Where otherworldly creatures skulk in dark woods and drift in the mist above marshes. Where Celtic musicians play the harp and pipe – making music that might flow like waves, breaking on the beach, or blow like summer breezes, caressing the headland. Places, too, where the telling of stories is an ancient, ancient craft.

Who can tell where the roots of these stories lie? The Celtic tribes began their long journey from the east some thousands of years ago, crossing central and southern Europe. As they followed the setting sun, they left behind their Celtic names for rivers, lakes and cities: from Lake Balaton in Hungary to Bologna in Italy and the River Douro in Portugal. Along the way they certainly shared and collected stories of extraordinary feats and heroes too. By now, Celtic culture lies on the edges of Europe – but its myths and stories live forever in its languages.

Museums and libraries across Europe hold and display many Celtic treasures – showing the love of colour and fine patterning that convey deep feelings within the simple images of their artwork. Songs and poetry, music and dance are at the forefront of their culture. And in their stories, we catch glimpses of their past and draw nearer to their temperaments and dreams.

Expect the unexpected in these stories, for magic and enchantment are a natural part of their characters' lives. Centuries ago, these myths and legends were written down in old books. In this volume, some of Wales's most experienced writers relate them once more, accompanied by magical illustrations from a talented new artist.

Now imagine it's the dead of winter, dark, with the smoke of an open fire and the storyteller's stirring words swirling about you …

Golden-headed Niamh

Golden-headed Niamh was fed up. There was nothing going on in Tir na-nÓg – the Land of Youth. In the rose garden, the sky was cloudless and the sun was shining – as it did every day. Bees danced between flowers, and everything was as perfect as ever. But Niamh longed for something to happen.

Her father was passing by. Seeing her, he said, kindly, "Niamh, apple of my eye, is there something wrong?"

"Yes, Father, there is. I'm fed up, and I want something to happen."

King Ri was alarmed. The whole point of Tir na nÓg was that everything was perfect, that everyone was happy and that no one wanted for anything.

"Hmm …" he said. "Why not go for a ride on your beloved white horse?"

Niamh smiled. Golden-shoe always lifted her heart. Suddenly, she had an idea. She stood up. "Good idea, Father, I'll do that," she said, skipping away.

In the stable, Niamh placed a saddle on Golden-shoe's back. Today was going to be different, she knew it. She said to the horse,

"We're not going to trot round the castle today, Golden-shoe. Today you have the perfect right to run free – to gallop just as you please. Off we go, my faithful horse!"

Golden-shoe whinnied and reared, throwing his hooves in the air. But instead of galloping, he skimmed swiftly overland, as if his golden hooves weren't touching the ground at all. They were moving at an amazing pace, and the wind was streaming through Niamh's hair. It felt magnificent. Soon the sea was before them but Golden-shoe sped onwards, above the waves. Niamh's heart was in her mouth – she hadn't expected *quite* this much of an adventure. In the middle of the sea was a green island and Golden-headed Niamh said she would like to land on it.

It felt so good to be on solid ground! And after their wild ride, there was something reassuring about trotting. As Niamh got her breath back, they passed through a wooded glade. And she realised that the sky above her head wasn't that blue. What's more, there was a slight wind blowing from somewhere, and a few of the leaves on the trees were gold and red, instead of green! This was a strange land indeed.

Turning, she saw a young man staring at her, and she pulled at Golden-shoe's reins to head towards him. The young man (who was very handsome, it must be said) was gazing at her, open-mouthed.

"Good morning," said Golden-headed Niamh, though she wasn't sure what time of day it was. "Where is this place?"

The young man swallowed. "This place? Um … this place is Erin …"

"And who are you, gentle youth?"

"Me? My name is Oisín. I'm the King of Erin's son."

The colour in his blushing cheeks deepened, until his face was like a rich, red rose. Golden-headed Niamh's heart leapt for joy.

"The king's son! That's fortunate. I'm the daughter of a king – the King of Tir na-nÓg. Can we be sweethearts?"

Oisín's face turned puce and, though he'd opened his mouth, not a word came out of it. But when she beckoned to him, he placed his foot in the stirrup to pull himself up and sit behind her in the saddle, holding tightly on to her.

"Home again," she commanded Golden-shoe. "We've had enough adventure for today" … And found a prince into the bargain, she thought.

After a magical journey over the waves, Oisín saw Tir na-nÓg appear beneath him. The Crystal Palace twinkled in the sun, its shining panes decorated with gold and precious stones. Silken banners fluttered in the wind and Oisín's happiness was complete. He could feel the golden tresses of this wonderful girl against his cheek, and he wanted to live with her forever.

Their feet touched down and they found themselves in the rose garden. Oisín looked about him as the sweet smell of roses came to his nostrils. He could hear the birdsong that filled the place, and the gentle hum of bees. Truly, this must be heaven!

They sat beneath a willow bower, Oisín staring, infatuated, at Golden-headed Niamh. He couldn't believe that such beauty was possible.

"How do you spend your time, Oisín?" asked Niamh, thinking she'd better get to know this young man, if they were to be sweethearts.

"Me? I'm a bard."

"A bard? What's that?"

"What's a bard?" said Oisín. "A bard is someone who enjoys finding the right words … someone who writes poems, and says things in song." He grabbed her hand.

"What sort of things?"

"Everything – beauty, betrayal, love, death, loss, rejoicing, the arrival and the passing of the seasons …"

Golden-headed Niamh had no idea what he was talking about, but then he kissed her, for that was what sweethearts were supposed to do.

"I have never felt so happy, Golden-headed Niamh," he went on. "I would love to live with you forever!"

Puzzled, Niamh asked, "What does 'forever' mean?"

"Forever? You know, till the end of time," said Oisín. This enchanting girl certainly had a strange way of flirting with him!

"But I don't know what time is," said Niamh, in distress.

"Don't look so sad," said Oisín, scratching his head. "It doesn't really matter. Time's just a way of measuring someone's age … from the time that they're young to the time they grow old."

But Golden-headed Niamh didn't know what 'old' meant. She shook her head. How could this boy be her sweetheart when she couldn't understand a word he said?

Oisín saw the pain on her face, and told her to forget everything he'd said. He wasn't a bard, and there was no such thing as time. There was no need to think about anything. The only important thing was to love each other, hold each other's hands while strolling about – and kiss each other. Such a life suited him down to the ground.

But, of course, such a life doesn't suit anyone for long. After a little while, Oisín began to feel ill at ease.

They happened to be in the rose garden one afternoon, and Oisín was studying the beautiful flowers. He'd become so used to their sweet scent by now that he hardly noticed it any more and, lately, the humming of the bees just got on his nerves. He was uncomfortable, and he was trying to remember the word from his own language that expressed how he was feeling. *Com*-something, was it? *Comhluadar?* – no, not that. Not *com*, but *cum*. *Cumha* – that was the word. It meant longing, and sadness, and homesickness.

"What's up, Oisín?"

"I have *cumha*."

"*Cumha?* I don't understand …" Golden-headed Niamh looked lost.

Oisín had forgotten not to use words that Niamh didn't understand.

"*Cumha* is something you feel when you remember how things were before …" he tried to explain.

But of course, Golden-headed Niamh didn't know the meaning of 'before'. In the end, Oisín kept things simple.

"Golden-headed Niamh, can I ask a favour? Can I borrow Golden-shoe today?"

Niamh agreed, as long as he came back.

"Of course I'll come back, as fast as I can," said Oisín. "I just want to see that my father is all right, and to show him that I myself am fine … I think I'll feel better then."

Oisín and Golden-headed Niamh stood with the horse before the gates of the castle.

"There's one condition," said Niamh, when Oisín was about to leave. "When you land on Erin's ground, be sure that your feet don't come out of the stirrups."

"What?" said Oisín. "You want me to stay in the saddle the whole time?"

Golden-headed Niamh nodded. "That's the condition. Don't set foot on Erin's ground. It's an easy enough condition."

She watched as her handsome sweetheart passed through the gates and Golden-shoe, given free rein once more, raced away like the wind. And that was the last she ever saw of him.

When Oisín reached Erin, he couldn't find his father's castle. All the passers-by he questioned stared at him in confusion. Then he came to an old man with a sickle, who was standing at the side of the road.

"Who are you?" asked Oisín.

"My name is Finn," said the old man. "Finn Clog mo Charran."

This had to be a lie. Oisín knew that Finn was Finbar and Mariread's little boy, a cheeky wee creature of two years old. Something was wrong here.

"And what about yourself, stranger?"

"I'm not a stranger. I'm Oisín – the son of King Seamus."

The old man turned and went on his way. What a tragedy, he thought. Only a young lad, but he's lost his mind already. King Seamus has been dead for years, and his son never returned … And all this well before the plague …

The only thing Oisín found familiar was the horizon. The shape of the mountains in the distance was the same, but nothing else made sense. He came to a heap of stones. A gang of old men were trying to lift one of them. Every face turned to look at him as he passed on his white horse, and they all looked wretched. Without thinking, Oisín got down from the horse and offered to help.

Suddenly, his leg gave way beneath him and pain shot through his back. The old men stared in surprise as Oisín reached out to greet them and saw the skin of his hand fall slack and wrinkled. He felt a beard growing from his chin, and saw that it was white as snow! What in the world was happening? Suddenly, through the fog in his mind, he remembered the warning – 'Don't set foot on Erin's ground' … but it was too late.

Back in **Tir na-nÓg**, a beautiful, golden-headed girl sits alone in a rose garden. The sky is cloudless and the sun is shining – as it does every day. Niamh knows very well, by now, the meaning of the word *cumha*.

Rhiannon and the punishment of being a horse

"The mounting block's over by the barn," said the farmyard maid.

She pointed to a stone platform where visiting riders could easily dismount from their horse after a long journey.

"Yeah, and you'll get a carry from there to the front door!" said a second maid, laughing into her sleeve.

"Don't refuse your lift!" said the first, a spiteful grin on her face. "There's mud and stinking puddles all over this farmyard. You don't want to spoil those fine leather boots of yours."

The stranger was surprised at this unsettling reception to the court of the Lord of Dyfed at Arberth. He was even more surprised as he approached the mounting block and saw the woman sitting on it. Her long, red hair had been braided down her back, like a horse's mane. She wore a tight leather cap around her crown, which was strapped beneath her chin. Reins had been attached to the cap and these lay at her nape. Over her shoulders and about her waist, more leather straps held something that looked like a saddle on to her back.

As he approached the mounting block, the woman stood and greeted him.

"Welcome, stranger. You may get down from your horse here. I will carry you on my back from the mounting block to the door. That is the punishment handed down from this court for killing and dismembering my child."

Despite her outfit and the unexpected words, the horseman knew that the woman who'd greeted him was a lady.

"You need not carry me," he replied. "I cannot allow that."

"I am Rhiannon, the wife of Pwyll, Lord of Dyfed," said the condemned woman. "Over four years ago, I gave birth to a son. The two of us went to sleep, with six maids to look after us. But when I woke in the morning, my face and hands were covered in blood. I had killed my baby. His bones were all over my bed … I do not protest my punishment."

The horseman turned to look in the direction of the maids-of-all-work, who were still watching from afar.

"Were those two maids amongst the six who watched over you and your son that night?"

Rhiannon nodded. The horseman nodded too, but he didn't say another word. At Rhiannon's heels, an old hunting dog, a bitch, howled in misery.

"What's wrong with the bitch?" asked the horseman.

"She has been like this since that night. She lost her puppies at the same time.

She has followed me everywhere since then."

The horseman saw the dog lick Rhiannon's hand. When he returned to his kingdom in Brycheiniog, he related the story to his companions at court.

Some months later, the account came to the ears of Teyrnon, Lord of Gwent Is Coed. He questioned the teller closely as to the time of the birth, then went home at once and called for his wife.

"Sad news from Dyfed," he said. "Pwyll and Rhiannon lost a son over four years ago. The same night … the same night …"

"The same night you came into my bedroom from the stable, carrying Gwri Wallt Euryn as a little baby, in your arms?" said his wife. "I have been preparing myself for this."

Every May Eve for years, Teyrnon's mare would drop a foal, out in the field. But, by morning, there'd be neither hide nor hair of the foal anywhere. Four years ago, it being May Eve, Teyrnon decided to take the mare to the stable and stand and wait, to see what happened. A fine colt was born to the mare but at once there was a great roar from outside and a huge claw came through the window and grabbed the foal. Teyrnon pulled his sword and cut the claw from the arm. The colt was saved, but a hideous scream came from outside. He rushed through the door and there, on the stone threshold, was a baby, wrapped in silken material. With the little bundle in his arms, he hurried to his wife's bedside.

"I've only been to the court at Arberth once, but our Gwri is the living image of Pwyll, Lord of Dyfed," said Teyrnon. "The same golden hair …"

"We have brought him up as the child we never had," said his wife. "But I knew that one day we'd have to return him to his parents. The silken material, that he had about him when you came from the stable – I knew then that he was related to highborn people. We must travel to the court at Arberth."

"We have no choice," said Teyrnon. "Rhiannon is being punished for killing the son that lives with us."

"We shall get three things for doing so," said his wife. "Free Rhiannon from her unfair punishment; share in Pwyll's joy when he finds that his son is alive and has been well raised by us – and also, if what I heard about Lord Dyfed is true, we shall have the honour of being foster parents to Gwri."

The next day Teyrnon started out with two companions and Gwri – who rode the colt that had turned four years old this May Eve – on a long journey across many saltmarshes and wide river mouths before arriving at Arberth Court.

"That woman killed her son and ate his flesh in her bed!" said the maid, who had just been milking. "Let her carry you from the mounting block to the door. A fitting job for the old jade!"

The maids were indignant that no one took up Rhiannon's offer to carry them, even when they'd heard her story. The companions from Gwent Is Coed went over to the mounting block.

"Welcome, strangers …"

Before Rhiannon could finish her story, Teyrnon interrupted her.

"Rhiannon, I know who you are. I have new information to share with you and your husband. Come with us – this is more important than any punishment the elders of the court have meted out to you."

Then he introduced himself and his retinue. He called to the farmyard maids to take the horses to the stable. They looked aghast to see the five of them, Teyrnon tenderly holding Rhiannon's arm, walk through the entrance door. The old dog licked Rhiannon's hand and followed them in.

Inside, various straight-laced officials tried to stop them, threatening the law of the land against them, but Teyrnon was not for turning. Before long, he was standing in the feasting hall before Pwyll, Lord of Dyfed, presenting himself and his companions. He didn't introduce Gwri – yet.

"Pwyll, I know that you are a fair and conscientious king," said Teyrnon. "You refused to divorce your wife, despite the evidence against her. I know how hard it is for you – never mind for her – that this seven-year punishment is upon you both. Not to mention the grief that the two of you feel for your son."

He went on to tell the account of the mare and the lost foals. He described the events of May Eve four years ago and finished by placing his hand on Gwri's shoulder.

"Pwyll and Rhiannon – I now know that this is your son."

For many, long moments, time froze in the hall. Then a shout went up from the crowd.

"Look at the likeness! No one could ever deny that the golden-headed lad is Pwyll's son!"

"If this is true, it will be the means to end my worry," said Rhiannon.

"That shall be his name! Pryderi!" cried Pwyll, joyfully, for, in Welsh, 'worry' is *'pryder'*. "That's the story of our son, exactly! And what better way to choose a name than to take it from the first words his mother uttered when she heard the good news about him."

The meeting turned at once into a celebration feast. Pwyll announced his deep gratitude to Teyrnon and his wife and appointed them as foster parents to the boy. He said that, for as long as he lived, he and his army would protect the lands of Gwent Is Coed. He tried to give precious treasures and the finest horses and hunting dogs as gifts to them. But Teyrnon would take nothing. He'd noticed one or two important officials sloping further and further towards the back of the hall during the feast, and he knew he had to say more.

"Some diabolical claw took your son from you four years ago," he said. "More than likely the same fiendish claw that snatched my foals, every May Eve. And, tell me, do you think it was the same claw that stole the pups from this old bitch, who never ceases to lick Rhiannon's hand?"

Silence fell in the hall. The nobleman from Gwent went on,

"If Pryderi was stolen, how came there to be blood on Rhiannon's hands and face the next day?"

The silence was shattered by the sound of a bronze pitcher, filled with ale and carried about the tables, crashing to the floor and resounding all over. By now, every eye had turned to look at the maid with the flaming cheeks. She wasn't one of the maids from the farmyard or the milking hall.

"I was one of the maids in the bedroom with Rhiannon and the little baby …" she said, her eyes nailed to the floor. "The six of us fell asleep before midnight, when we were supposed to be keeping watch over the mother and child …"

"You will not be punished for telling the truth," said Pwyll.

"I was the first to wake … It was early morning and Rhiannon was still sleeping … I looked for the baby – but there was no sign of him! I shook the others awake and the six of us searched high and low, but in vain. What on earth were we to do? Then one of us – and I won't say which one – said that the hunting dog had just given birth to a litter of pups. Very quietly, we went to steal them from her, killed them and smeared blood over Rhiannon's face and hands, placing the bones in her bed with her. And that's the truth that has troubled me ever since then and that's the truth that led to Rhiannon's vile punishment … Her word against the six of us, it was, and they say that six are always closer to the truth than one …"

The old she-dog gave a soft little whine and lifted her head to lick Rhiannon's hand for the very last time.

Ker Is

My name is Ahez. Mine's an old story … a sad one, a mad one and a rash one – if you ask the Bretons of today. This is what they sing about me:

> *'Ahez, merc'h ar Roue Gralon,*
> *Tan ân ifern ên he c'halon.'*

which means:

> 'Ahez, King Gralon's daughter
> Hell's fire in her heart.'

But *I'm* telling the story now, because I want you to hear my side of it.

I come from a place called Ker Is, which means 'Low Fort' – because my city and the fertile fields around it lay on low land claimed by my people from the sea, with strong embankments and locked floodgates to prevent it flooding at high tide. Although there's not a trace to be seen of Ker Is these days, I whispered my story to the waves and now, from the depths of the sea, flow these words …

Ker Is was once the richest and most luxurious province in all Brittany. The city itself was full of everything anyone could ask for and more, and its people enjoyed all the costliest things in life – from silken clothes to sumptuous food and drink. Surrounding Ker Is and stretching into the distance were bountiful grounds where wheat, fruit and vegetables flourished, with grasslands to feed plump bullocks, sheep and swine. The people of Ker Is were so wealthy that having plenty of money was no longer something fortunate, to be thankful for – but rather something to be taken for granted.

In the main court at Kemper, the capital of his realm, King Gralon, my father, worried that the people of Ker Is had lost sight of all that was important in life. Rather than looking after one another and thinking of others' welfare, the endless wealth in that city by the sea had caused its people to do nothing but gather more money, more food and drink, more gold and silver.

To escape these troubling thoughts, Gralon gathered a troop of his best knights and out they galloped to hunt in his forests. But though they sought the kingdom's most fruitful hunting grounds and saw many deer, they failed that afternoon to catch even one.

As night began to fall, they decided to try again in the morning. But as the sun's light waned, finding a sheltered spot to spend the night proved more difficult than expected. And so they split up to search for a suitable place. All at once, one of Gralon's men came across a lone cottage in the middle of the forest. He saw smoke lifting from its chimney and the light of a little candle in its windows. A good sign, he thought to himself, as he rode swiftly back to Gralon. When the troop reached the cottage, a man was waiting for them on the doorstep. King Gralon asked the man, whose name was Kaorentin, if he and his knights might shelter there for the night.

Without hesitation, Kaorentin agreed, welcoming the king and his troop, urging them to take off their coats of arms and to feel at ease.

Kaorentin could see that they were famished after their long ride and their efforts to hunt. And so he suggested that some of the knights accompany him on a foray to gather the ingredients for a feast. At this, looks of disbelief grew on the faces of the king and his troop. How could this man, who owned nothing more than a candle and the roof over his head, hold a feast for them all?

Kaorentin led a handful of men towards a river-pool not far from the cottage, collecting a leaf or two of herbs on the way. When they reached the pool he turned to the knights and asked if they were ready to carry the feast back to the cottage and the king. The knights gaped at each other in surprise, for all they could see, circling in the pool, was a single little fish. Kaorentin asked to borrow a knife from one of them. Then he reached into the water and the fish rose up through the pool, as if it was coming to him of its own accord. Kaorentin cut the tiniest piece of flesh from the fish's belly before lowering it again and letting it swim away, completely unharmed.

"Give me a sack to carry the feast back to the cottage," said Kaorentin. The knights laughed in his face, but they threw a sack to the crazy man who thought this tiny bit of meat would feed a mouse, never mind a band of hunters. Kaorentin ignored their insults, leading them back to the cottage. By the time they'd opened the sack before the king, out fell a heap of fish on to the table. Enough to feed the whole, hungry troop, and to provide a meal worthy of a king. The men apologised for ridiculing him earlier and Gralon, together with every single knight, thanked Kaorentin for such a fine feast.

The following morning, my father insisted that Kaorentin came with him and his men to the court in Kemper. Then Gralon travelled on to Ker Is, where I tried to welcome him with a feast and a *fest-noz*, which is a night of singing and dancing. But my father was not in good spirits. He complained of this and that, while claiming that 'the situation was even worse' than he'd expected. That's how he was for the days, weeks and months to follow. I could do nothing to lift his heart or change his downhearted

expression, though I offered him gifts and hosts of merriments and entertainments.

I listened to him addressing his closest court counsellors. "My people, the privileged citizens of Ker Is, do nothing but feast, carouse, sing and dance – then complain the next day that they have over-feasted, over-caroused and over-danced, before doing the same thing all over again the following night." I completely agreed with my father but, unlike him, I knew there was no changing the people of Ker Is. My father believed, in vain, that his own good example would make them alter their way of life and cause them to be more grateful.

In order to set such an example, and also because he no longer trusted anyone but himself to do it, my father took over the responsibility of protecting Ker Is by guarding the floodgates in the huge embankment that kept the sea from drowning the region. I offered to help him with this task, but I was brushed aside. My father's endless ill humour knew no bounds.

One night, at the end of my tether, I decided there was only one way to wake the people of Ker Is from their stupor. All my father's dutiful actions, all his comings and goings with the key to open and close the floodgates, had no effect on anyone. Everyone continued to carouse, to feast, to live ungratefully then complain about their luxurious lives.

So I set about giving them a little warning of my own. To show them how it might feel to be threatened by the incoming sea …

The feeling of power that flowed through my veins then was astonishing. I headed straight to the embankment and fitted the key – stolen, from my father's bedroom – into the floodgates' keyhole and turned the heavy latch. As I wound and twisted the mechanism to lift the gates, I could see the moonlit water starting to stream in over the land. My plan was to give them just a taste of the end of the world. But there was no end to the water, and I, on top of the embankment, could no longer do anything to stop it. As the sea flowed and flowed on to the lands of Ker Is, a strange feeling came over me. I could hear music in the waters, I began to dance, and a wave of freedom overcame me …

From the embankment I saw lights appearing in castle windows as candles were lit in the court, and I half-heard, through the sea's breaths, voices, shouting at each other.

I imagined the scene: Gralon finding me missing and waking the court, and everyone searching everywhere, in vain – no sign of a thief or a pirate anywhere. Then one of the watchers from the castle tower running to my father, crying breathlessly, "My King! The distant floodgates are open and the tide is rising! And what is more, your daughter, Ahez, is to be seen, dancing on the crest of the embankment. She is in great peril. We are all in peril. The sea has already begun to drown the fields around the city."

My father: "We must make haste to close the flood doors. Or the whole of Ker Is will disappear beneath water!"

"It is too late, Gralon." Kaorentin appears, suddenly, in the king's court.

"Kaorentin? But I left you in Kemper …? From where …? How …?"

"There is no time to explain. There's no time to close the floodgates, either. You and your people must flee at once. That is the only hope for the citizens of Ker Is. Follow me back to higher ground."

"What about Ahez? Call my horse! I must rescue her from the embankment."

"Impossible. I am very sorry, Gralon. You have to know that all this is your daughter's work. She opened the floodgates."

"Ahez? That surely cannot be … But … how … why?"

"We must hasten, or drowning will be the fate of all of us," Kaorentin replies.

Gralon gallops wildly through the city of Ker Is, shouting to everyone to leave,

shouting that the sea is coming to drown them. The water is already seeping into his horse's hoofprints. But no one flocks to follow him and flee. Instead, Gralon sees his people loading their expensive bric-a-brac, their fine clothes, their gold and their silver, on to carts.

"Come, Gralon, before it's too late!" Kaorentin shouts.

Gralon hastens to follow Kaorentin, a look of disbelief on his face. Though the water has risen to his waist, his people are not troubling to come with him. Instead, they are still loading their worldly goods into carts and sacks.

The king cannot understand the folly of his people, even of his own knights, as he and Kaorentin ride as swiftly as they can towards high ground and safety. Between every breath he thinks of me, his daughter Ahez, unable to understand why she has done what she has. Perhaps I myself will never be able to explain why either, but everything happens for a reason, so they say.

When the two of them reach ground high enough that the sea no longer chases them, Gralon and Kaorentin turn and look back. There is nothing to be seen of the wealthy city and the fertile lands that were once Ker Is. There nothing any longer but the open sea, stretching to the horizon, and the whole
thing – the city, the people, and I, Ahez, among
them – has disappeared beneath the waves.

Morag the Clever

I was scared out of my wits when I woke up. I was in a tidy little kitchen with little chairs and a wooden table, tiny little saucepans hanging from hooks, and a little man standing in front of me.

"Who are you? And where am I?" I asked, angrily.

"Morag," he replied, "you're in the King of the Fairies' kitchen. You have been chosen to be Royal Baker. This special honour has been granted by the king himself, for it was you who made the most delicious breadcrumbs he's ever tasted. Now you will stay here forever. Start your work at once, if you please. The king has declared he would like bread for supper."

"But I don't want to be here," I said. "And I certainly don't want to be here forever. Why me? And how did I get here in the first place?"

The little man, who turned out to be a butler, explained that a troop of fairy soldiers had stolen breadcrumbs from my kitchen, and that the king had been enchanted by their taste. So they'd put a spell on me to make me fall asleep and carried me here, leaving my baby behind in our cottage, all on his own. What a thing to do! And who in the world was this King of the Fairies, to tell me, Morag, what to do? I know lots of women who'd have lost their tempers or wept in this situation, but I knew better than that. I counted to ten under my breath and I had a think. What could *I* get out of all this? How could *I* profit from this greedy king and his demands? There'd be benefits in baking for a king, for sure, but I didn't want to leave my home – I was happy in our humble, bare little cottage. There had to be a way to please these fairies and to fool them at the same time. They say that fairies are hard to fool, but not for an old hand like me, Morag Redhead. And woe betide anyone who tries to fool *me*!

"You're not getting any bread till you bring me my baby," I said. "The poor little thing's at home, all on its own."

"Fine," said the butler, and he called the fairy troop.

As they set off for my house, I had another think. To help the ideas flow, I stamped my feet on the floor and drummed my fingers on the table.

"Stop making that noise!" said the butler. "The king can't stand noise.

Fairy ears are very sensitive, you know."

The king's stomach will be very sensitive too, if I poison his bread, I thought. But I smiled nicely at the butler. When the baby arrived, safe and sound in his cradle, he was ready to be fed. I took my time to feed and nurse him. At last, he went to sleep.

"Get to work now," said the butler.

"There'll be no baking till I get my spoon and my mixing bowl," I said, with another smile.

"Everything you need is here already," replied the butler, heading for a cupboard.

"I can't make bread without my own things," I insisted.

The butler harrumphed and sent the fairy troop back to my cottage to fetch the mixing bowl and the spoon.

"There'll be no baking till I get my jug and my rolling pin," I said when they got back with the bowl and the spoon. "I can't make bread without my own things."

"Fine," sighed the butler. "But you must start baking after that."

The fairies came back with the jug and the rolling pin. But I still wasn't satisfied. "How can I make bread," I asked, "without eggs or flour or milk? You fairies must go back to my cottage and fetch them for me."

With much frowning and grumbling, the fairy troop returned to the cottage once more. When they'd gone, I had another idea. I started whistling through my teeth, annoyingly. The butler told me to be quiet and went rushing off to check that the king hadn't been disturbed. Peeking after him, I could see the Fairy King himself, asleep in a nearby room.

You should have heard the little fairies complaining as they struggled through the kitchen door carrying a whole urn of milk! And perhaps rolling the eggs up the hill hadn't been the best idea … for they were covered all over with yellow yolk.

"Get baking now, Morag," ordered the butler, impatiently.

"All the king had for breakfast was breadcrumbs – he'll be starving by now."

The king's got a nerve, I thought, to complain about eating breadcrumbs – when they were stolen from my cottage behind my back! Anyway, I began to make the bread, hoping my plan would work. I poured and I mixed and I beat and I folded, banging dishes as I kneaded and squeezed the dough. The butler was watching me anxiously.

"Must you make so much noise?" he hissed. "If the king is disturbed, we'll all be turned into frogs!"

Suddenly I had a thought.

"I'm sorry," I said, "but I feel rather upset. I can't help thinking about my animals – there's no one at home to feed them and stop them from straying. You must bring them here." And I stopped work and sat down in the biggest chair with my arms folded in front of me.

"I can't do that!" exclaimed the butler. "Where would we put them?"

"That's your problem," I replied, leaning back against the cushions and breaking into song. 'Follow my Highland Lassie' echoed through the kitchen.

"Shush! Be quiet!" pleaded the butler. "All right. I'll do my best. Just don't make that din again."

"Din indeed!" I replied. "I happen to be singing a lullaby to my baby." Then I stopped singing and pretended to be asleep.

Once again the fairy troop were put to work. And what a tough time they had of it! At last they returned – with seven sheep, six lambs, five chickens, four kittens, three cats, two dogs and a little yellow duckling – all squashed together in the palace kitchen. What with all the clucking, barking, mewing, quacking and bleating the baby woke up, of course. And screamed his head off.

"Stop that noise!" begged the butler. "If the king hears, he'll turn us all into mice! Shut the baby up!"

"For that I need my husband Duncan's help," I said. "He'll be walking home now, from Aberdeen Fair. You fairies can meet him on the road and bring him here."

The butler clicked his fingers to call the fairy troop. But, "No!" they shouted as one. "We're worn out. We're too tired to lift a finger."

"Oh dear. Then I can't bake any bread," I said. "I can't do another thing until Duncan steps into this kitchen."

"All right, all right! I'll fetch him myself!" said the butler.

Out he went, all hot and bothered. I poked at the fire to warm the oven with a quiet little smile. My plan was working. I washed up my baking things and wiped the table clean, and before I knew it it was time to feed the baby again.

I'd just finished when Duncan came in. Dropping his bagpipes in surprise, he stared at me.

"What's happening? What's going on here?" he asked, amazed.

"I'll explain later," I whispered in his ear. "Now play a tune while I finish making this bread. And play as loudly as you can!"

So Duncan played his pipes. At first they made a little bit of a sigh and then they made a little bit of a drone, then 'Scotland the Brave' wailed out across the kitchen.

The baby shouted and clapped his hands. The fairies screamed. The sound of the bagpipes shook the whole palace, making the housekeeper wail and run from the kitchen, knocking the butler to the floor. Then Duncan began to sing 'Scots Wha Hae', very loudly, as I put the bread dough into the oven.

The door crashed open and the king stepped in. His crown was hanging over one eye and his fists were clamped to his ears.

"Out!" he shouted. "Out, out, out! Out before I turn you all into snakes! Scarper, every one of you! I never want to see you again!" He grabbed the mixing bowl and the rolling pin and threw them out the door. Next moment the jug and the spoon came flying after them.

I grabbed the baby and Duncan grabbed the cradle.

Gathering the rest of our stuff as we went, we set off for home – with seven sheep, six lambs, five chickens, four kittens, three cats, two dogs and one little yellow duckling. As we walked, I told Duncan the whole story.

"Clever Morag," laughed Duncan. "Only you could fool the fairies!"

The next morning, the fairies came into my kitchen with a message from the king. He was sorry for everything that had happened – but my bread was still the best he'd ever tasted. If I were to leave a little piece of it out for him every week, I'd be well rewarded. And so, ever since then, I leave a slice of bread on the window sill at the northern end of the cottage. And every week it disappears, and a little piece of gold is left in its place.

My cottage kitchen isn't so humble and bare any more. Duncan still plays his bagpipes at Aberdeen Fair. I'm happier and wealthier than I've ever been, doing what I've always done – baking bread. And woe betide anyone who tries to fool Morag Redhead again!

THE GIANTS OF KARREK LOOS YN KOOS

Once upon a time, when magic and enchantment wandered the earth, a husband and a wife lived in Marghasyow in Cornwall. But they were no ordinary husband and wife – Kowrmoran and his wife Kowrmelyan were giants!

Although Kowrmoran was one of the strongest giants in the world, he was a lazy old creature and it was poor Kowrmelyan who had to do all the work. It was she who'd skin the animals for supper, she who'd fetch seawater to fill Kowrmoran's wash-tub, she who'd build the mound of stones to throw at local people; she who did everything!

One day, as he was reclining on an enormous boulder and watching Kowrmelyan ripping up trees by the roots to make their fire, Kowrmoran had an idea.

"You know, Kowrmelyan," he said, "I've had enough of lying awake at night, worrying that the Cornish people are about to attack us."

"Oh?" exclaimed Kowrmelyan, confused. "But it's us that attack them! You're forever stealing their cattle and sheep!"

"Be quiet, will you – I've had a great idea."

Kowrmelyan's heart sank. She knew that Kowrmoran's great ideas meant more work for her – from first thing in the morning to last thing at night.

"I want you to build a tall hill in the middle of the sea," said Kowrmoran, "so that I can see right over this thick wood to the village. Then I myself will build a castle on top of the hill, where I can lie in a huge bed and keep an eye on the people of this area. Away with you now! On with the work!"

Kowrmelyan couldn't believe what she was hearing, but she knew there was no point disagreeing with her husband so off she went, head bowed, to gather heavy rocks before carrying them in her apron to the middle of the sea. Kowrmelyan worked tirelessly through rain and shine, walking back and forth, back and forth, day after day. Slowly, the pile of stones grew into an island and then a hill and, throughout all this, Kowrmoran didn't lift a finger to help. He simply shouted instructions, pointing here and there with his oak-trunk staff.

By the end of the summer the hill of stones could be seen from afar, and Kowrmoran was delighted.

"Kowrmelyan!" he bellowed one morning. "You can stop carrying stones now!"

"At last!" said Kowrmelyan, sitting down in exhaustion. "I've got painful blisters all over my fingers."

"But there's no time for rest!" Kowrmoran yelled. "Go and get our furniture and carry it over to the hill. It's time for us to move house!"

Once again, Kowrmelyan obeyed her cantankerous husband and dragged all their belongings from the damp cave where they'd lived for centuries. When she'd finished, Kowrmoran sprang through the sea towards the hill with his staff slung over his shoulder. It was time to create the biggest castle in the world. A castle that would be the envy of everyone, from Cornwall to Cymru! But one thing was for sure, Kowrmoran wasn't going to build the castle himself. Oh, no – he was far too lazy for that.

Kowrmoran could perform magic, and he'd been saving up all his powers and spells for years now, for this very occasion. He got to his feet and thrust his staff up into the air before closing his eyes tightly and roaring the words,

"May all of my magic and all my spells unfurl
To conjure me the finest castle in the world!"

Over on the shore, the villagers were enjoying their lunch when suddenly came the blast of a huge thunderbolt, filling the air and shaking the earth. Everyone ran out of their houses in fear and when they looked out to sea, they couldn't believe their eyes! With his staff, Kowrmoran was busy drawing a magnificent castle down from the clouds and placing it on top of a hill in the middle of the sea! They looked at each other, completely flabbergasted. How in the world could a castle descend from the sky?

The villagers watched as the two giants left the land for their new home. Then they began to feel a wave of relief. Perhaps the giants would leave them alone, now that they had a grand castle to live in? Perhaps Kowrmoran and Kowrmelyan would be respectful and peaceable neighbours now, like everyone else?

Respectful and peaceable? Kowrmoran and Kowrmelyan? Not likely! Before the villagers could go back inside and close their doors, Kowrmoran was striding back through the sea towards the village, staff in

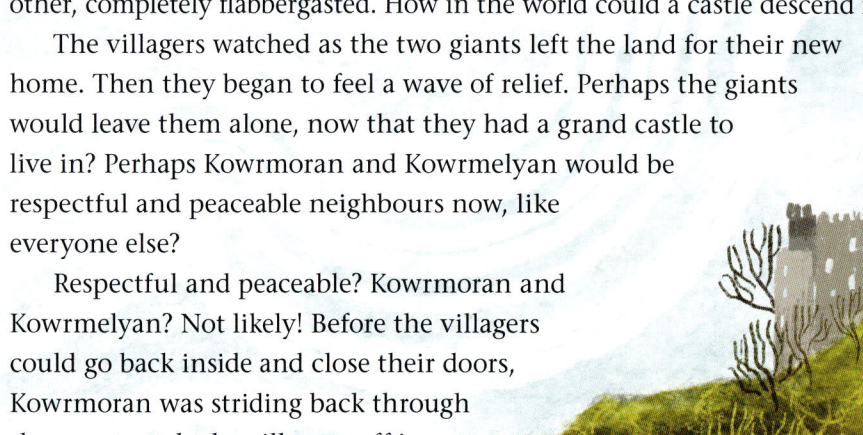

hand, to search for food. There was no respite for the villagers at all and, as the days went by, Kowrmoran and Kowrmelyan's behaviour got worse – no two ways about it. Every day they'd storm into the village and terrify everyone and everything. After grabbing three or four cows, tying their tails together and throwing them over their shoulders, and stuffing a handful of sheep into their sacks, they'd return to their castle on the island. This happened every single day, until the local people were almost out of their minds.

One afternoon, all the nearby villages came together to hold a meeting. Everyone, from Porthia to Penn an Wlas, had had it up to here. They knew they'd be starving before winter if Kowrmoran and Kowrmelyan carried on like this. So they decided to offer a large sum of gold to anyone who could get rid of the giants. But when they asked for volunteers, the crowd fell silent.

Until, suddenly, a young boy raised his hand.

"I will challenge the giants!" he said, full of confidence. "I'm Jakka, from the village of Ding Dong. I think I can stop old Kowrmoran and Kowrmelyan's antics once and for all."

The villagers looked at each other, very unsure. Could such a young person really defeat the giants? What hope would Jakka have against two such villainous creatures as Kowrmoran and Kowrmelyan?

But Jakka was determined to give it a go, and he started planning at once.

That night he crept on to the beach with a spade and began to dig a hole in the sand. In no time the pit was deeper than Jakka was tall, but he kept at it, burrowing and burrowing for hours. He dug so hard and so determinedly that he felt as if his back was breaking. But, in the end, he was satisfied with his work. He climbed carefully from the pit, placed a long, thick piece of wood over its mouth then sprinkled sand across the whole thing.

"Ha!" said Jakka. "Now no one will guess there's a huge pit under there!"
And he sat quietly nearby, to wait for sunrise.

When dawn broke, Jakka saw Kowrmoran at the door of his castle, yawning so loudly that it shook the birds from the trees. Fear shot through Jakka when he saw the size of the giant. For the first time, he began to have doubts about his plan. After all, he didn't want to be Kowrmoran's breakfast that morning! But then he pulled himself together and breathed in deeply before yelling at the top of his voice. Kowrmoran's head swivelled straight towards the mainland to see what was making the noise.

"Who in the world dares to challenge me, first thing in the morning like this?" he said, mad as a hornet.

But Jakka didn't stop. He kept on shouting and jumping up and down. The next thing he knew the giant was thundering towards the beach, heading straight for Jakka and waving his staff in the air. Kowrmoran was about to give Jakka a whacking when, at the last moment, Jakka side-stepped and Kowrmoran fell headlong through the wood and into the pit. Before Kowrmoran had a chance to think, Jakka snatched his sword from his belt and cut the giant's head clean off. His plan had worked!

"Thank goodness," sighed Jakka, proud of himself. Then he turned to see that all the people of the village had come out and were jumping for happiness on the cliffs above his head.

But suddenly, everyone fell silent. Who was galloping through the sea from the island but Kowrmelyan the giantess. Oh no, thought Jakka. I forgot about her!

As Jakka turned on his heel and sprinted from the beach, he could have sworn that Kowrmelyan was smaller than he'd remembered. He rubbed his eyes and saw that yes, she was – and what was more she was getting smaller and smaller with every moment. Suddenly, Jakka realised that the enchantment that made Kowrmoran and Kowrmelyan dangerous giants had been broken when he'd cut Kowrmoran's head off. Now, with every step she took, the water came higher and higher towards Kowrmelyan's head until, by the time she'd reached the beach, she was no bigger than a tiny mouse! Before anyone could catch her, a gull flew down and closed its claws on the scruff of her neck, and Kowrmelyan was never seen again.

The villagers were overjoyed that Jakka's cunning plan had worked. Who'd have thought that such a young boy could have beaten the biggest giants in the land! No less a person than the Mayor of Penzance, Marazion and St Ives came to present Jakka with a sack of gold, and it was announced that a magnificent feast would be held that night, to celebrate his feat. In the middle of the party, Jakka was given another special present, a silver belt. On it were the words:

This is the bravest boy that e'er was known –

Slayer of the giants that terrorised our homes.

He wore the belt for the rest of his days, and from that moment on he was known as Jakka the Giant-slayer.

And what of the hill that Kowrmelyan built in the middle of the sea? The Cornish people named it Karreg Loos yn Koos, which means Grey Rock in Woodland. It's also called St Michael's Mount – and you can still see it there today.

THE MERMAID OF PURT LE MOIRREY

Purt le Moirrey is a little village which lies lazily on the shores of the Isle of Man. Long ago, most of its inhabitants were fisherfolk, well used to the creatures of the briny sea – the fish, the crabs … and the mer-people.

For some weeks now Sam Collister had felt someone watching him when he was out fishing. His mother, Ealish, had dismissed his worries to begin with. But when he started coming home and saying that a girl with hair like spun gold had been following his boat, Ealish began to worry that a sea she-creature had taken a fancy to her son.

The people of Purt le Moirrey were well used to stories about the mer-people. Stories of fishermen, led into peril on the seas; stories of being pelted by fish; stories of tempting treasures, left too close to the waves to be fetched. The best thing to do, with the mer-people, was to ignore them. Ealish remembered a tale from when she was a child, about one of Purt le Moirrey's young fishermen. He'd been charmed into the sea by a mermaid – or a *ben-varrey*, as they're called on the Isle of Man – and had drowned, leaving his poor mother with her heart broken in pieces.

It was not long before the *ben-varrey* was making mayhem once more. That day, Ealish found the front step covered in seaweed and dead crabs. She flew into a rage. Grabbing the shovel from the coal shed, she scooped up the lot of it and threw it over her little garden wall onto the rocks, so the sea could swallow it again. And that's when she saw the golden head, rising from the waves.

"Get out of here, you she-devil!" she cried in fury. "There's no welcome here for you, with your evil enchantments! My Sam isn't interested in you. And if I see one more dead crab or piece of stinking seaweed on my doorstep again, I shall stuff the lot of it down your gullet! You hear me?"

As the mermaid wailed and disappeared beneath the water, Ealish stared out to sea. Already she regretted her angry words. When she came back into the house she found Sam sitting at the table with his head in his hands.

"What have you done, Ma? You know that no good comes of cursing the *ben-varrey* like that. I'll not catch another fish again now!"

Sure enough, from then on, every time Sam went out fishing he came home empty-handed, complaining to his mother that the mermaid had followed his boat, singing louder than ever to try to catch his attention. What with poor Sam having to keep his eyes fixed on the horizon so as not to look at her, and holding his hands over his ears so as not to hear her, he was quite unable to cast his nets.

One day, Ealish had had it up to here. She decided the best thing to do was to seek a special spell from the wise woman who lived up the nearby hill. This wise woman offered enchantments and potions to help the people round about. Her name was Pyee Kerruish and she, like many others, knew about Sam Collister's troubles with the beautiful *ben-varrey*.

She said to Sam, "You'll need all your seaman's strength to deal with a *ben-varrey* like this one. Take a necklace of glass pearls and a silver comb with you, and make sure you wear your mother's wedding ring. A *ben-varrey*'s beauty is her biggest weakness – these gifts should keep her quiet for a bit. Stand strong, hold the gifts in your right hand and raise your left hand into the sky, so she can see the wedding ring. Say these words:

*Ben-varrey, ben-varrey, away with you home.
To calm you I give you these pearls and a comb.
See you this ring – I'll not marry thee
'Til the shores of our island take leave of the sea.*

Then throw the gifts into the water."

That night, as the full moon scattered silver on the still sea, Ealish gave her son a necklace of glass pearls and a silver comb. Then she placed her wedding ring on his finger and off he went in his fishing boat.

Sam shivered as the night breeze crept over him. Then, he heard something moving in the water by the boat. He stood up nervously and the mermaid appeared, her golden hair shimmering in the light of the moon. Sam gazed at her before closing his eyes tightly and reaching into his pockets for the pearl necklace and the silver comb.

She began to sing. Her lovely voice set Sam Collister's soul a-tremble. Rushing to say the words before her voice enchanted him completely, he stammered,

*"Ben-varrey, ben-varrey,
away with you home.
To calm you I give you
these pearls and a comb."*

But because he was trembling so hard and racing so quickly through the rhyme, he forgot to say the words exactly as Pyee had told him to …

*"See you this ring –
I shall marry thee
While the shores of our island
are joined to the sea."*

He threw the necklace and the comb with so much strength that his mother's wedding ring slipped from his finger. Like a flash of golden lightning, the mermaid sped to catch it, slipping it on to her own finger. Then, lifting her shining tail from the water, she waved it in the air in triumph before disappearing into the depths.

At the exact moment the ring fell from his finger and the words from his tongue, Sam had decided that being married to a mermaid wasn't such a bad idea after all. And, by the time he got home to his mother he had a love-struck grin on his face.

"Well? Did you get rid of the little vixen?"

"No, I didn't. I think that marrying a mermaid's a good idea, Ma. She's beautiful, she's lovely – and I want to live under the sea with her," said Sam, dreamily.

"What's wrong with you, you oaf? You'll drown, for sure!" Then Ealish realised he wasn't wearing the wedding ring. "Oh no, Sam Collister. What have you done?"

"Found me a wife, Ma …"

"Why ever would you want a wife with a tail? She enchanted you, with her deadly voice …!"

For days after this, Sam sat on the rock outside the house, gazing out to sea. Ealish couldn't leave him on his own for a moment, for fear he'd get into the water.

He didn't say a word, or do any fishing any more. Things were pretty bad, all told, what with the mermaid calling for him every evening with her songs, the light of the moon dancing on her golden hair and shining in Sam's eyes.

But Ealish Collister was a determined woman. So she marched back up the hill to seek help from the wise woman.

"Well, it's very difficult to undo a spell when there's a wedding ring in the mix," said Pyee, pouring them both a cup of herbal tea.

"By heaven's fishes – we have to try something!" Ealish cried.

"Hush now – I'm a-thinking." Then Pyee went into her pantry and came back with a little pot.

"Herring eggs," she said, handing it to Ealish. "Boil them for three days then crush them fine like flour. Put the powder in Sam's food, when he's having his supper.

"The same night, someone must take Sam out in the boat, carrying the plant they call holy herb, or vervain, with them. When the *ben-varrey* appears, they'll need to throw the herb into the water and repeat these words:

Ben-varrey, ben-varrey, away home with thee.
'Til the shores of our island take leave of the sea.
Sam can't marry you, no matter your wishes
If he did, for sure, he'd drown with the fishes."

There were yet more instructions after this. Ealish had a lot to remember as she ran home with the herring eggs in her pocket and the words of the spell swirling in her head. She couldn't afford to forget a thing.

The first step was to boil the eggs for three days, crush them and put them in Sam's supper. She managed this with no trouble, for Sam was so distracted he didn't notice anything his mother did. Next she taught him the rhyme – making sure he recited the words correctly this time. Then they went out in the little fishing boat, with three of Sam's friends to help them.

Suddenly, the mermaid leapt from the water, shaking her golden hair at the moon, and Sam jumped to his feet calling, *"Ben-varrey, ben-varrey –"*

Before he could say another word, his mother shouted, *"Away home with thee!"*

Then Sam joined her to say:

"'Til the shores of our island take leave of the sea."

And the two of them finished the spell, once and for all:

*"Sam can't marry you, no matter your wishes
If he did, for sure, he'd drown with the fishes."*

One of Sam's friends threw the holy herb into the water and the other stabbed the sail with a knife and whistled for wind, just as the wise woman had instructed.

Ealish knew that whistling for wind on the sea was very dangerous. She reached for her son and clasped him tightly in her arms.

A storm raged, hurling the fishing boat landwards like a leaf on the wind.

The mermaid screamed in fury and thumped the water, whipping it with her tail until she'd stirred up huge waves. Ealish heard something clink against the boat's hull but it wasn't until they were thrown back up on shore that she saw what it was. By her feet lay her wedding ring. Sam picked it up, and Ealish held her breath. What would he say, after all this mayhem?

"Ma?" he said, placing the ring on her finger. "This belongs to you."

They stared out across the peaceful sea, following the silvery path of the moon. There was no sign of the wind, the waves, or the mermaid.

From that night on, the *ben-varrey* was never seen again at Purt le Moirrey, and Sam Collister lived a long and happy life with his mother. When Ealish Collister died in old age, he dwelt by himself in their little house by the sea. The word 'batchelor' was carved on his gravestone, so they say. I don't know if that is true, but you could do worse than go and have a look, the next time you're on the Isle of Man.

AN EYE FOR AN EYE AND A TOOTH FOR A TOOTH

The lands of Connacht stretch across much of western Ireland, and many legends from the age of the Celts are still told there today. One of them is the story of Maebh, the Queen of Connacht. But if you think of queens as noble ladies who sit around in grand rooms and sew all day, you'll need to think again. In Celtic times women held positions of strength and respect in society, and wealth gave equal status to kings or queens. This wealth was often counted in the animals they owned – especially cattle. And that's the basis of the story about the battle that took place when Maebh tried to steal the bull called Donn Cúailnge from Cooley in Ulster.

Maebh was an exceptional person and, according to legend, she had magical powers. She was strong and determined, and she'd never let anyone get the better of her. She was beautiful and gifted too, with a close connection to the natural world and the earth, and it's said she could run as fast as a horse. But Maebh was also jealous and fiery-tempered and, like many characters in old Celtic tales, she left a trail of trouble and destruction behind her through the lands of Ireland.

Because Maebh was so beautiful, countless men fell head over heels in love with her and she was married several times. Her first husband was Conor, the King of Ulster. But Conor wanted a quiet, obedient wife – the complete opposite to Maebh. So she left her husband and went back home to Connacht. But then Conor married her sister, Eithne. Maebh wasn't happy about this at all so, when Eithne was expecting her first child, she had one of her servants murder her. But the child – a little boy – survived, and he was named Furbaide.

Maebh went on to marry a man called Ailill, making him the King of Connacht. But before long Maebh had had enough of Ailill too and had fallen in love with a young soldier from Ulster by the name of Fergus Mac Roich. Soon Maebh and Fergus were openly courting each other and Ailill became very angry.

One stormy night, Maebh and Ailill were arguing and soon Ailill was bragging about his wealth and achievements. Now, there was one thing that got on Maebh's nerves more than anything, and that was her husband trying to say he was better – or richer – than her. No one was allowed to be wealthier, stronger or better at anything than Queen Maebh – especially not Ailill.

"There's no doubt that I'm much stronger than you," said Ailill, pushing out his big belly. "I'm much wealthier than you too, so that makes me a lot more powerful."

Well, Maebh wasn't about to let this go unchallenged.

"Of course you aren't!" she snapped. "How can you be richer than me? You had nothing until I agreed to marry you."

"Yes I am – I'm much wealthier than you."

"No you aren't."

"Yes I am."

And the two of them argued like this for some time, boasting and comparing their wealth in gold, fine wine, weapons and silver plate. Then the quarrelling went on to list all the animals they owned – sheep, goats, cattle …

"You have nothing that I don't have more of," said Maebh, noticing the smirk on Ailill's face. For he had one treasure up his sleeve that he knew would bring the argument to an end.

"Oh, but I do," said Ailill, very pleased with himself. "I have Finnbennach, the great white bull, and he's worth a fortune! Do you have anything like him?"

Of course, Maebh flew into a fury at this. She had nothing to compare with Finnbennach the white bull and, because cattle were the most valuable possessions of those times, this made Ailill very rich indeed. And that made Maebh's blood boil. She wouldn't be satisfied now until she herself owned a bull as strong and mighty as Finnbennach, so she sent servants the length and breadth of Ireland to search for a bull that would compare with him.

Soon, another bull was found. He was one of the bulls of Ulster, and his name was Donn Cúailnge. He was very powerful, exactly what Maebh was looking for. She sent her wisest men to Cooley to bargain for him and, before too long, the owner agreed to sell him to Queen Maebh. But as they were leaving, the owner heard two of the men discussing how they'd have stolen the bull if he hadn't agreed to sell it to them.

This enraged him, and he changed his mind. He was keeping the bull after all – and he sent Maebh's messengers home empty handed.

Well, this wouldn't do at all, so Maebh gathered together her troops and, without a second thought, marched her army, with Fergus at her side, to the province of Ulster to steal Donn Cúailnge the bull. But Ulster's armies were ready for her – and they were prepared for a long and bloody battle.

At first, so the story goes, Queen Maebh was triumphant in battle, for she had cast a spell on the Ulster soldiers – a spell that made them fall down and roll in pain, too weak to lift their weapons and defend their *cúige* – their province. Just one of Ulster's troops could withstand Maebh's magic, and he was a young man by the name of Cúchulainn. According to legend, he himself had magical powers, powers that made him as strong as Maebh. Cúchulainn was also friends with Fergus – the two of them had known each other since childhood – so they refused to fight one another. And Cúchulainn managed, single-handedly, to defend Ulster against the army of Queen Maebh, slaying soldier after soldier in the middle of the river as the enemy tried to cross it. This battle went on for many months, with Connacht's best men falling under Cúchulainn's hand.

Some time later, the spell on the men of Ulster lifted. At last they regained the power to fight and, gradually, Ulster succeeded in conquering Connacht's army, forcing Queen Maebh to retreat and turn for home. But she hadn't forgotten the reason she'd gone to war months earlier and she was still dead set on getting hold of Donn Cúailnge, the bull from Cooley. So, on her way back to Connacht, she managed to steal him. Then she drove him and her army home to show the animal to King Ailill.

"Look! Look!" said Maebh, as soon as she reached the palace. "Look at my bull, he's a hundred times better than your white one!" She laughed in triumph.

At that moment came a terrible sound from the fields, and everyone rushed to see what was happening. They saw the new bull, Donn Cúailnge, and the white bull, Finnbennach, fighting furiously. The fields of Connacht weren't big enough for two bulls the like of them. After a dreadful battle, Finnbennach was killed, but not before goring

his enemy. Ailill and Maebh watched as the white bull fell, and then Donn Cúailnge, though wounded, got to his feet and galloped back towards his own lands in Ulster.

The king and queen stared at each other in astonishment. All that ferocity and all that bloodshed had been in vain. Not only had two fine bulls been lost but, much worse than that, many young men of Ulster and Connacht had lost their lives – and all because of a quarrel between Ailill and Maebh.

Things went from bad to worse between the king and the queen after that. Ailill was furious to see that Maebh and her lover Fergus were still strolling shamelessly about, hand in hand, under his very nose. One day, when Fergus and Maebh had set off for a walk in the woods, he summoned one of his young archers.

"Come!" called Ailill. "Hurry! I have just seen a young deer over there, between the trees. It will make a fine feast for us tonight, if you can shoot it with your bow."

Of course, it wasn't a deer at all, but Fergus in his coat of animal skins. The archer notched his arrow, aimed and pulled back the bowstring – "Whiish!" His aim was true and the arrow struck Fergus, felling him, dead, at Maebh's feet.

Maebh knew at once who was responsible, and she wasn't about to forgive her husband. In no time she'd taken her revenge. One morning, one of the palace servants found the king with a knife through his heart.

Maebh had led a wild and violent life. She'd succeeded in keeping her power and status as the Queen of Connacht, but there was no escaping her troubled past. After the deaths of Fergus and Ailill, life quietened down a little for her. Every day she'd go to bathe in a beautiful pool on the outskirts of a settlement called Sligo. But, unbeknownst to her, someone was watching her, biding their time and measuring the distance between their hiding place and the pool. This person practised with his sling until he was certain that his shot would be strong and true.

Furbaide – for that was who it was – knew that his aunt Maebh was responsible for his mother Eithne's murder, all those years ago. He'd waited a long time for this opportunity. And so, one day, he hid once more amongst the reeds at the edge of the pool, waiting for Maebh to get into the water to bathe. Furbaide fitted a piece of hard cheese into his sling, threw back his arm and fired.
The missile shot through the air and hit Maebh on her forehead, killing her instantly.

According to legend, Maebh was buried on a hill called Cnoc na Ré near Sligo, facing towards Ulster. Even in death, Maebh is ready and waiting to face her enemies once again.

Rhos y pawl

"Clear that soot from the fireplace, you lazy hussy!"

"I'm sorry, Father," said Aeronwy, kneeling at the hearth and starting to sweep.

"And where's my breakfast? Here I am, slaving away in those fields, and no sustenance to be had. D'you expect me to graze on grass, like an animal?"

Aeronwy turned to her father and her eyes were damp with tears. She hated it when he blamed her unfairly.

"But Father! I made you a bowlful of porridge this morning, just as I do every day. It was ready for you as soon as you got up …"

Her father grabbed her by the arm and squeezed it, painfully.

"Don't you dare answer me back, understand? Bowlful of porridge indeed – you think that's enough for a man like me, with lambing time upon us? That was hours ago … I'm starving hungry!"

Aeronwy knew better than to argue. She brushed the ashes from her dress and stood up to go to the kitchen.

"Where d'you think you're going, you great slattern?"

Aeronwy sighed. His voice was like a sledgehammer in her head, that never stopped …

"To make you something to eat, Father …" she said, wearily.

"And leave this room in such a state? Finish your chores before starting a new one – how many times do I have to tell you?"

He got up and went to the door.

"Keep your food; I don't want it. You've upset me – like you always do. You can't make a decent meal for the life of you anyway – you're no better than your mother. I'm going out for a bit of peace."

And he slammed shut the door.

Thank goodness he's gone, thought Aeronwy. She could only ever relax when the house was empty. When her father was under the same roof she was on tenterhooks – there was no knowing when he might turn on her and beat her. And why did he have to talk about her mother in such a scornful way, her having passed away? That hurt Aeronwy more than anything.

She finished sweeping the fireplace and arranged heather and firewood in the hearth, ready for this evening's fire. Not that she could bear to sit by the fire if her father was in the same room. She'd rather slave in the kitchen or clean the house or be out of doors – anything to be out of his sight.

Aeronwy's life would have been unbearable if it weren't for one thing. She had a sweetheart – a boy from Gelli Ffrydiau. She loved nothing better than to remember their first meeting.

Aeronwy's home was Talymignedd, a farm on the level land at the furthest end of the vale of Dyffryn Nantlle by Drws y Coed – you can still see it there today.

From her house, she could see the crests of the mountains and feel them watching over her – Craig Cwn Silyn, Mynydd Talymignedd, Trum y Ddysgl, Mynydd Drws y Coed, with Yr Wyddfa, in all its splendour, at their very centre. But the mountain opposite was her favourite – Mynydd Grug. A girl of the great outdoors was Aeronwy, only truly happy when rambling in the mountains. She was forever crossing the river to gather heather on Mynydd Grug, and her favourite spot was the lake called Llyn y Ffynhonnau. This was a very special place. When her mother was pregnant with Aeronwy, she'd come here – not surprisingly, for it was so very tranquil. By this lake, Aeronwy felt peace, and sometimes she'd gaze into the water's depths and talk with her mother.

One day when she was at the lake's shore, a tall young man came by. He had wavy hair that fell to his shoulders and a fine, strong figure. His eyes were dark as night and a touch of sorrow glinted within them. Cam was his name and, after they'd conversed a little, he did something completely unexpected. He kissed her. Aeronwy had not felt such affection and tenderness since her mother had died. She and Cam became sweethearts, and they wished to be together forever.

It was their custom to wave to one other every evening before turning in for the night – Cam standing on Craig y Bere and she on Clogwyn y Barcud, on the other side of the river. A little ceremony, confirming that their love burned true.

Time after time, Cam asked her father for Aeronwy's hand in marriage, but the farmer from Talymignedd would hear none of it. Take his only daughter? How would he live then – with no one to feed him and look after the house? Let the scoundrel go elsewhere to find someone to marry – he wasn't going to steal Aeronwy!

After a year of this, Aeronwy knew that something had to change or she would surely go out of her mind. One January night of heavy snow and a wind that howled and swirled down the vale, she asked her father for the hundredth time whether Cam could marry her. She had prepared a particularly tasty meal for him, and had given him the last of the beer from the new year's barrel. In the grate a warm fire roared. He didn't seem in too much of a bad mood, so she dared to ask the same old question, just in case.

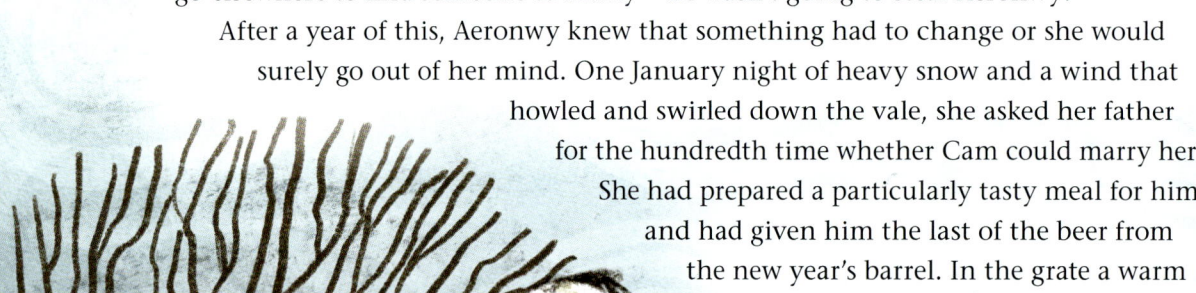

"I've been thinking about this," replied her father, wiping his lips on his sleeve and breaking wind, "and I've decided to let you two be together …"

Aeronwy's heart leapt. What, in the wide world …? Was her father drunk? Could she really dare to dream of a better life?

"… on one condition." There was a gleam in his eyes and, looking into them, Aeronwy could see the reflection of the fire's flames. It occurred to her that he was raving mad.

"Anything, Father. You know that Cam would do anything to please me."

"The boy must prove he's fit and worthy. He must show me his mettle. I've thought of a task, and it's as simple as you like. All he need do is stand on the rhos above his house – through the night. And he'd better not cheat – I'll be keeping an eye on him."

Aeronwy didn't know what to think. It was a simple enough task, to be sure. Then she looked through the window and saw the snow falling … thick, fine snow. She knew it would be quite a feat to stand up on the rhos, which means moor in Welsh, through the long hours of the night, surviving a storm like this.

"That's all?" she asked, nervously.

"That's all. If he's still alive by morning, he may marry you."

Aeronwy got to her feet.

"I'll go over and tell him. Perhaps he'll want to choose a night that's less rough than this one …"

Her father hadn't expected her to take him seriously. He looked through the window himself.

It was a stormy night, to be sure, but perhaps there was still a chance the rogue would survive it.

"He must complete the task tonight," he insisted, then his mouth curled into a sneer, "and don't forget to tell him to take off every scrap of clothing … or he'll have none of you."

He'd lost his senses – no two ways about it.

"Father, what's wrong with you? That would be certain death … Could even you live with the consequences?"

Her father stared into the fire. "I've told you the conditions. It's up to him to decide how much he loves you. But if he doesn't accept the challenge, you two'll see no more of each other."

Aeronwy stepped through the door and closed the latch. She should have known better than dare to hope. She struggled through the storm to Craig y Bere and, through her tears, she told her sweetheart his task. She also told him the consequences. Cam's face paled. He knew that this could be his last night.

Quietly, between kisses, Cam told Aeronwy to go home, to stay awake and to keep a candle burning in her window so its tiny flame would keep his hopes alight …

Cam needed one further thing, and he knew exactly where to find it. Near Gelli Ffrydiau there was an old iron pole, or pawl. He went to get it and to fetch a sledgehammer. On the rhos above his home he took off his clothes, stood the pawl on end and began to strike it with all his might. The ground was hard and he was afraid it had frozen solid, but eventually he forced the tip of the pawl into the earth. Strike … strike … strike … It seemed an impossible task. The cold ate into the very marrow of his bones, as if thousands of needles were piercing his nerves. There had never been a night as cold as this, he thought. But it wouldn't do to stand still.

Strike … strike … strike … and, with each blow, he knew that the day of deliverance was drawing near. All he had to do was keep striking – strike … strike … strike … And dawn was approaching … Strike … strike … strike … and his dream was coming true. Down in the vale, a little candle was burning, and beside it the face of the girl he loved. Strike … strike … str– He felt lightheaded, and darkness closed about him.

No one was more glad to see the dawn break across Clogwyn y Barcud than Aeronwy. She hurried over the river, a pack containing a woollen blanket on her back. The sound of striking metal had stopped, and she feared the worse. What if …? She didn't want to imagine anything so dreadful. She didn't want to live in a world without Cam. As she ran towards the rhos, she saw the sky above turn ghostly pink. The colour deepened, as if an unseen hand had stabbed it. Then it spread until it had painted a dawn the like of which she'd never seen. And then she saw the pawl, dark against the white background of the snow. It was now a low stump before her. And by its side lay the naked body of her sweetheart.

"Cam!" she screamed, running towards him, the pack with the blanket falling to the ground.

"Cam?"

He lay still, and the skin of his broad back was blue with cold. She fell to her knees and tried to turn his body over. His eyes were closed, and snow dusted his eyelids.

"Cam …" she said, and felt her tears flow.

She kissed the frozen lips and cried his name, over and over.

Then came a miracle. Cam's eyes opened. She saw two dark gems, and from these flowed the most resolute love she'd ever known.

"Aeronwy …" he whispered, and Aeronwy knew that her very deepest hope had come true.

To this day, this piece of land is known as Rhos y Pawl.

The Daughter of the Waves

A quiet worker, not given to conversation, was Roderick MacCodrum. Fishing was his trade, and he farmed a bit of land too, on one of the islands of the Hebrides.

Roderick and his older brother had learned about the sea and its secrets from their father. Every day, he knew in which direction to row his little boat and where to drop his net or throw his fishing line. The two had also learned the songs and stories of the waves from their mother, and Roderick knew that some of these were as old as the stone walls of his cottage.

But there was a tragedy at sea. A ferry, sailing between two islands, sank in rough weather, and Roderick lost his parents and his brother. After this, he lived alone in a straw-thatched cottage not far from the sea.

Roderick kept himself to himself. He wasn't one to go from house to house of an evening, telling stories and singing songs. He'd be on his own in his boat by day and likewise kept his own company by night. He was content with this, and no one ever thought to ask if he was a lonely man. No one ever wondered whether he was a happy man.

After supper one night, he'd closed his eyes and was dozing on the settle before the peat fire. An hour or so later he awoke and got up, deciding to go outside for a stroll, so as to make sure he'd sleep well in his bed, later. It was a fine night and the moon was bright. He walked, taking his time, along the beach where he kept his boat.

There, by a stone that was covered in periwinkles, he stood, stock still. Over at the far end of the beach he saw a group of tall, graceful young people, dancing and laughing in a ring. Their hair whipped in waves about their shoulders and their eyes shone. He marvelled at their long arms and legs, which they shook hither and thither in a lively, merry dance. One of the girls – who had long, flowing dark hair – was singing a song that was entirely beyond his ken. A magical song, full of the sea's movements and the secrets of the deep. He knew who they were. His mother had told him about the children of the sea.

He stood out of sight behind the periwinkle stone, taking pleasure in the scene, held spellbound by the singing. Moving an inch, his foot touched something soft and smooth behind the stone. He bent to lift it, and saw that it was the skin of a seal. Looking down, he could see in the light of the moon that there was a whole pile of seal-skins. Some grey, one or two black, and one bright gold, like the sand on the beach.

He lifted the light skin and saw it shining in his hand. It felt soft against his cheek. Something to remember this special night, he thought. He turned for home and, heading towards the peat fire, he put the skin away above the joist of the window which looked out to sea.

Before very long, he heard a light knock at the door. When Roderick opened it, he saw the young girl with big, soft eyes that were as dark as a peat-pool in summer. She wore not a scrap of clothing, but her black hair reached almost to her waist. Her body trembled and there was fear in her voice.

"Have you seen my seal's skin?"

"Seal's skin?" asked Roderick.

"It's light-coloured. Have you seen it, if you please?"

"The tide comes in quickly," said Roderick. "Perhaps the tide has washed it out to sea."

The fisherman pulled off his cloak of tartan wool and placed it over the girl's shoulders.

"Perhaps the tide will bring the skin back to the beach tomorrow morning," he said then. "Or the late tide, perhaps …"

The girl looked at him with her big eyes. Eyes like the bed of the sea, thought Roderick. A lie is always obvious, thought the girl.

"There's fish soup over from supper. Come. Take some, to warm you."

The girl stayed in the cottage that night. First thing in the morning, she went out

to the bay and searched the waves for the sealskin that was golden as sand. Much later, Roderick saw her walking back to the cottage, head bowed.

Word went about the island that Roderick MacCodrum had found himself a girl from over the seas, to be his wife. Her ship had sunk and the fisherman saved her, said some. She ran away from a cruel mother, said others. However, everyone agreed that it was a good thing he had company at last. A wife's the best thing that could've happened to him, they said. Oh, she's a quiet enough lass, of course – so they'll suit each other down to the ground.

After many a tide had ebbed and flowed, children were born, and these grew to be such a boy and a girl as to warm their father's heart. They had big, shining eyes, like their mother. The sea takes; and the sea gives back, Roderick thought, remembering his brother and his parents. And, this time, he was very grateful that the sea had changed his life for the better.

The sealskin was never mentioned after that first night. His wife never complained, never reproached him. So different to some of the other island wives, thought the fisherman. He believed her to be content enough. But every high tide he noticed her leave the cottage and go out on to the beach, to gaze long and longingly at the waves.

By the peat fire, the mother taught her children to sing some of the beautiful songs of the sea. These were songs which filled the cottage with uncanny feelings – sometimes joyful, like the sea's laughter; sometimes melancholy, like the cry of the waves against rugged rocks on a foggy night. Roderick told his son and daughter some of his own mother's stories. But he avoided the one about the children of the sea.

The day came when a hare crossed the fisherman's path as he walked to his boat on the beach at break of dawn. He was in two minds whether to go back to the cottage or not – it was an ill omen for a hare to cross your path in the morning. But on he went. Pushing the boat out into the gently lapping waves, he jumped in and began to row for the fishing beds.

He hadn't pulled in his first cast of the net when coarse drops fell upon his hands from the black clouds above. Looking towards the horizon he saw more low clouds, driving fast in his direction. The storm broke before he reached shore.

Back in the cottage, the mother and children heard the wind, snarling in the big chimney. The daughter went to the window to watch for her father, but the rain was so heavy she couldn't see the waves, let alone the fisherman's boat.

Suddenly came a gust of wind that was mightier than any in this wild storm. Pieces of the thatched roof above the sea window were ripped away and the little cottage filled with the roars of the wind, which threatened to tear the whole roof off.

"Fetch a rope from the barn and throw it over the ridge of the roof from the back of the cottage!" shouted the mother to her son. "Tie the end of the rope to the anchor at the back. I'll catch the other end and tie it to a table leg."

The son made several attempts before managing at last to get the end of the rope into his mother's hands. By now she was standing on a chair in the teeth of the storm, her head out of the hole in the roof, watching the rope being thrown to her over the

roof's ridge. Once she'd made sure the roof was as fast as could be, she climbed back on to the chair to tidy the roof-straw, as best she could, above the window.

That's when she saw what had been hidden from sight, many years ago. She took hold of the soft, golden skin, and lifted it to her cheek. She closed her eyes. She could not move, though the storm whirled about her.

"Ma! Ma! Are you all right?" Her son's voice was full of concern.

The wife climbed down from the chair, placing one arm around her son's shoulders and the other around her daughter's. She said not a word against her husband, who had hidden the sealskin for so long. She didn't speak about his lie. She didn't recall the dark hours on the beach; all she remembered was the love and happiness they'd shared in this cottage, and she kissed the two children, over and over.

Opening the door, she struggled against the wind to make it down to the beach. There, as the waves leapt like white horses along the sand, she pulled off her earthly clothes and put on the sealskin. She jumped into the spray, throwing one last look at the cottage before swimming for the open sea.

She sang a song of the wild waves as she swam out of the bay. From somewhere, she heard faraway songs in answer. She knew that her family were waiting for her. She leapt forward, her heart racing.

On his way in from the open sea, Roderick MacCodrum gave thanks that the little bay was in sight by now. He had made it through tempestuous, perilous waves. He heard seals singing and barking and he looked up from his oars for a moment to see the head of a seal, bobbing above the waves, very close to his boat. Shining eyes, bright with longing, looked at him. Eyes full of tenderness, eyes full of pain.

Then the seal dived beneath the surface and the fisherman caught a glimpse of golden skin, like sand on the beach on a peaceful day.

He rowed wildly for shore. Rushed along the path to the cottage, seeing the hole in the roof and the rope that was holding down the rest of it. Before he opened the door, he knew that only the children would be there waiting for him.

Through their tears, he heard the whole story. He took them in his arms and sat with them on the settle by the peat fire. He told them his mother's story about the children of the waves – about the old witch that turned the sons and daughters of the King of the Sea into seals, fated to drift forever with the currents from one island to the next. Only on rare, moonlit evenings could they venture from the sea, on to some remote shore. He sang them the song he'd heard on the beach when he'd stood by the periwinkle rock.

Most of all, he taught his children never to hurt or harm the seals of the islands of the Hebrides – for the children of the sea share the same blood as the children of the land.

THE ADVENTURE OF KERESEN OF SEN SENAR

Once there was a young girl called Keresen who lived with her family in a cottage on the cliffs near Sen Senar in Cornwall. But though she loved to help her parents with their work on the land – growing vegetables and keeping animals – she wasn't quite happy. For every time she came home from the fair at Morvedh, she'd complain to her mother that all her friends wore beautiful dresses, and she had none.

"But Keresen, love," her mother would answer every time, "you know that we're much too poor for that."

This went on until Keresen couldn't bear to stay at home, dreaming of fine clothes, for one second longer. She announced to her parents that she was going away to find work as a maid.

"Goodness gracious!" said her father, fearfully. "Whyever aren't you happy here, with us?"

"I'm sick to death of having to wear these rags, Father," answered Keresen. "I promise I won't go far, and I'll come back home with a pile of the most beautiful frocks in the land!"

And with that, Keresen gathered up her belongings and said farewell to her beloved family. Her mother clasped her hand, tenderly.

"Be careful," she said. "Strange people wander that road. Come back to us safely, and soon."

Keresen had never imagined that leaving home would be so difficult. She'd hardly reached the next hamlet, Gōn Arlodhes, before she began to feel homesick. Then, suddenly, she heard footsteps behind her, though she was sure no one had been there a moment before. She turned, and there stood a tall man, dressed in fine clothes.

"Good morning!" said the gentleman.

"Good morning, sir," answered Keresen, shyly.

"And where might a young girl like you be going this fine day?" asked the man.

"I'm looking for somewhere to work as a maid," answered Keresen, and the man smiled from ear to ear.

"Well isn't that a piece of luck," he said. "My name is Rudhek, and I was on my way to look for someone to come and keep house for me! You're the very person."

Rudhek chattered non-stop about this and that and seemed so pleasant that Keresen didn't notice she'd been following him for miles and miles. On and on they went, until they reached a narrow path that led to a colourful garden. In its centre stood an enormous mansion.

"My dear Keresen," said Rudhek, pointing at the mansion, "behold, your new home!"

Keresen cried out in wonder. This place looked as if it belonged in the world of magic and enchantment!

Then a little boy came running from the house and leapt straight into Rudhek's arms. Fast on his heels was a grim-looking old woman.

"Don't worry," whispered Rudhek, seeing the fear on Keresen's face. "That's Aunt Aggie – she's decent enough, though she's rather a grump!"

Before Keresen could open her mouth, Aggie began to list her duties as a maid.

"Now then," said Aggie. "There are some very important tasks you must perform each morning. At the break of day, take the boy to the spring in the garden and wash him in its water. Then, find the crystal casket that's hidden in a crack in the nearby rock. Open the casket, rub the ointment inside it on the boy's eyes, but never, ever, touch your own eyes with it."

"But …" began Keresen, confused.

"Be quiet!" interrupted Aggie. "Lastly, you must go to the cow, milk her and give a bowlful of the milk to the boy, before returning to the mansion."

Keresen had never heard of such an odd set of tasks before, but she said nothing, for she didn't want to aggravate Aggie.

"You will sleep in the boy's room," Aggie went on, turning on her heel, "but you will not open your eyes or say a single word throughout the night. Understood?"

"Understood," answered Keresen, bewildered.

Though Keresen hardly slept that night for thinking of Rudhek, the boy, Aggie and her strange orders, she dared not open her eyes until dawn broke. Then she took the boy straight to the garden and followed her instructions to the letter; washing the boy, rubbing ointment on his eyes, milking the cow and giving the boy a bowlful of milk. Then the two of them walked back to the mansion, perfectly happy.

However, Aunt Aggie wasn't in nearly such fine spirits, scowling at Keresen as she gave out the rest of the day's chores.

"And remember," she said, after reciting a long list of housework, "even if you finish all your duties, you are not to wander the mansion and its grounds. And you are most definitely not permitted to open any locked door."

Keresen nodded, knowing she'd be very foolish to go against Aggie's orders. Then she got straight on with her tasks.

Keresen loved her work at the mansion, but it soon became obvious that Aggie didn't like her friendship with Rudhek. Keresen happened to be cooking one morning when the older woman shocked her by striking her across the back with a broom handle. Luckily, who was to come through the door at that moment but Rudhek himself.

"Pack your bags, Aggie," he said in fury, "and return at once to Nancledra!"

Keresen couldn't believe that she was now mistress of the house, and a whole year passed in the twinkling of an eye. She and Rudhek understood each other perfectly and lived together more like two friends than master and maid.

But though she continued to work obediently, Keresen longed to know what was so special about the ointment she rubbed on the little boy's eyes. One morning, when Rudhek was away and the boy was asleep, she crept into the garden and rubbed a little of the ointment on to her own eyes. She knew at once that she shouldn't have touched it, for her eyes burned like fire. Rushing to the spring she splashed water on them to ease the pain, but then she noticed something moving beneath the surface. There, at the bottom of the pool, were tens of tiny people, playing happily together. And who should be in the middle of the crowd but her master, Rudhek!

"How in the world can Rudhek be at the bottom of the pool?" Keresen thought to herself, alarmed. "The ointment must be a magic one. Now I can see little people in every nook and cranny of the garden!" For the tiny folk weren't just in the water, they were everywhere.

Keresen adored the gorgeous dresses of the little women, and she crouched down to get a better look. Then she saw that a group of them were heading towards a black stone at the base of the garden wall. One of them began to recite a rhyme.

*"O black stone, fairest stone of all
Reveal the treasures of the garden wall
Trencrom!"*

Suddenly, the black stone slid aside and the tiny women entered a cave full of priceless clothes and precious jewellery. But before she could study these in detail, Keresen began to feel sick. It dawned on her that she'd broken one of the important house rules and that, from now on, she'd have the ability to see wonders like these.

"How will I hide this from Rudhek?" she wondered. "When he's been so very kind to me?"

The next morning Rudhek left the mansion, saying he was going out to hunt. But when Keresen went into the garden she could see him clearly once more at the bottom of the pool, no bigger than a little finger. She saw him go towards one of the tiny women – a woman more beautiful than all the rest. Then Rudhek kissed her! Jealousy shot through Keresen and, all at once, she knew that she was in love with her master. She felt her heart break there and then, and she fled to hide in her room for the rest of the day.

When she heard Rudhek arrive home, Keresen opened her door a crack to see where he went. He disappeared into one of the rooms and then she heard the sounds of singing and laughter, flowing from under the door. Daring to put her eye to the keyhole, she saw her master enjoying the company of his new sweetheart once again. Keresen looked sadly down at her own ragged clothes and realised the cruel truth – she would never stand a chance of winning his heart, despite all her dreams about grand dresses.

When he greeted Keresen the next morning, Rudhek could tell at once that she wasn't herself. Then he noticed the traces of tears on her cheeks.

"What is wrong, dear Keresen?" he asked.

"Don't speak to me!" cried Keresen. "Go back to the little people and your sweetheart!"

Rudhek's face paled and all signs of the warm feelings he had for her vanished from it.

"You have used the ointment!" he exclaimed. "You must leave at once!"

At this, he clicked his fingers and disappeared into thin air.

Keresen was afraid, knowing that her adventure in the amazing mansion was over. She collected her things and began to walk, head bowed, down the garden path. When she reached the gate she heard footsteps behind her and there stood Rudhek, sadness in his eyes.

"Though I am angry with you," he said, "I don't want us to part like this, what with us being friends. You may not return here for a long, long time, but I have a feeling we'll see each other again some day."

Rudhek handed Keresen a present and she tore it open eagerly. Inside, beautifully wrapped, was a pile of exquisite dresses – far lovelier than her friends' and lovelier even than those worn by the little women. But when she lifted her head to thank him, Rudhek had vanished once more.

Unable to wait a moment longer, Keresen took off her rags and pulled on the loveliest dress of them all. She walked home, her mind in turmoil and, by sunset, she could see her cottage in the distance. Neither her mother nor her father could believe their eyes when they saw who was walking down their path, for years had passed since Keresen had left home.

"You said you'd return in a fine frock, didn't you Keresen?" said her mother, hugging her tightly. "You look finer than the queen of the fairies, you do indeed."

Keresen was content enough for a good few weeks, but then she began to tire of being home and she'd escape by night to climb Trewey Hill and walk towards Gōn Arlodhes. There, she'd wander the byways for hours in the hope of seeing Rudhek – but she'd make sure to be home before dawn, with her mother waiting eagerly for the sound of the latch.

And then, one full moon night a year to the day after returning to her parents, Keresen crept from the cottage wearing her very best dress. And although her mother waited patiently for her, no one heard the lifting of the latch in the little cottage in Sen Senar, and no one saw Keresen ever again.

The Story of Gráinne

For many, this will be a story about power. The power of a father over his daughter. The power of traditions and customs over freedom. The power of envy. The power of forgiveness.

For me, it's about more than that …

My father, King Cormac Mac Art, had arranged for me to marry Fionn Mac Cumhail, leader of the Fianna. This was more than I could stand. I was a beautiful young girl, clever and gifted – only a really special person would be right for me. And Fionn Mac Cumhail wasn't that person! My father wanted Fionn on his side, because Fionn was such a great warrior. Well, why should *I* have to suffer because of that?

I first saw the right person one fine morning, when the sun had just risen over the Hill of Tara. A band of young men had gathered to play a game of hurling. One of them was stronger than the rest, striking the hard ball long and far. I had never seen such a beautiful man in my life, and I decided then and there that he was the one I would marry.

After that, I couldn't stop thinking about him.

I longed to see him again. I had no idea what his name was, but I felt sure I could persuade my father to send someone out to find him. I was wrong.

"You are to marry Fionn," he said.

"I will not," I answered.

"Everything has been arranged. And that's an end to it. It's I who decide."

I argued my case, but my father would not give in. One hideous morning, he forced me from my bed. Made me wash. Made me put on a beautiful robe that had been chosen for me by someone else. I was decorated with colourful gems. Then I was dragged to my own wedding.

I looked about the hall, searching for a chance to flee, for someone to help me escape. A group of men, accompanied by a hunting dog, stood laughing and conversing by the fire. One of them looked in my direction and I felt myself turn weak. It was the hurler. I came to know that these men were the Fianna, Fionn's soldiers, that Bran was the name of their dog and that the hurler was called Diarmuid O'Duibhne. I realised that I was in love with Diarmuid O'Duibhne.

I called for my maid.

"Fetch the fine drinking horn from my room," I whispered, "and fill it with wine. Then add this." I pulled a sleeping draught from my pocket.

"Give the cup to Fionn first – tell him that Gráinne has sent it. He will pass it to others. But watch carefully to make sure that the Fianna do not touch a drop."

The maid obeyed and, as the company drank, they fell asleep, one after the other. Seeing this, the Fianna became anxious, some reaching for their weapons. They paused as I crossed the hall and stood before Diarmuid.

"Diarmuid O'Duibhne," I said. "I order you to help me. I refuse to marry Fionn Mac Cumhail. You are the one that I love. Take me from this place at once."

The Fianna stepped back, and Diarmuid looked into my eyes.

"I cannot help you," he said. "You are engaged to be married to Fionn Mac Cumhail."

"My father arranged this wedding without my permission. You must help me escape."

"I cannot," said Diarmuid. "I would rather spill my own blood than betray my master."

"Diarmuid O'Duibhne, I place you under royal command. Help me escape from here."

"Very well," he said. "Come, Gráinne." And, taking my hand, he led me out into the darkness.

We walked for hours before reaching a forest, where we collected wood and branches and made a small, sturdy cabin. And so we spent our first night together – unmarried, lying lovingly on a bed of rushes to the sound of late birdsong. I had never felt more happy. Diarmuid confided in me a story, that an enchantment had been put upon him when he was very young. According to the enchantment, a wild boar would one day kill him. The story sent a shiver down my spine.

The next morning, we awoke to hear a dog scratching at our wooden walls, barking and howling. Diarmuid knew at once that it was Bran, the Fianna's hunting dog. Bran loved Diarmuid O'Duibhne more than anyone in the whole world. Now he had found us, and Diarmuid knew that he was in danger.

We managed to escape that time. But we were always in danger, always on the run. Fionn followed us everywhere. One day Aengus, Diarmuid's godfather, came to us and said that he had a message from the king – my father. He and Fionn had decided to forgive us for everything, and asked that we give up hiding and come home. After years of wandering, Diarmuid too had had enough.

"We can't live like hunted animals forever. Shall we accept your father's invitation and go home? They have forgiven us now, after all."

I asked Aengus to tell my father that we agreed. Enough water had passed under the bridge, and now we could all of us move on and live happily. However, I had still not forgiven *him*, by a long way. But my father consented to the plan and promised that he and Fionn would leave Diarmuid and I in peace.

We went to live on the land of the O'Duibhne clan, building a house there and calling it Rath Gráinne. We had four sons and one daughter, and we were so happy. But one thing still worried me. Every time Diarmuid went out to hunt, I'd live in fear, with the story of the boar forever at the back of my mind.

I told this to Diarmuid.

"Perhaps we need more protection from your father," he said. "If you were to see him and to welcome him as part of the family, you'd feel safer. What about inviting him here?"

"What about inviting Fionn Mac Cumhail too, while you're at it!" I replied, hotly.

"That's not such a bad idea." Diarmuid laughed.

Then he persuaded me that forgiving the two of them was the right thing to do. Woe is me for agreeing to such a thing.

My father and Fionn arrived one afternoon – the king with his men, Fionn with the Fianna. They spent a year at Rath Gráinne, feasting and hunting. I was glad that at last my family were together; it was a pleasure to see my father with his four grandsons and granddaughter. Fionn was very old by now and, for his part, he seemed happy enough to make peace.

But there was a storm brewing on the horizon.

Late one evening came the sound of a hunting horn through the darkness. Diarmuid started from his sleep.

"Someone is hunting on the mountain of Ben Bulben!" he cried. "I must go and join them."

"Take your best weapons," I said, as Diarmuid armed himself.

"I'll take my light ones," said Diarmuid. "I'm only going out to see what's happening – I don't intend to fight."

Kissing me lightly he stepped out into the dawn.

Only later did I learn the story from the Fianna. Diarmuid went to Ben Bulben. There he met Fionn Mac Cumhail, who stood alone with Bran at his side.

"The Fianna have been hunting through the night," said Fionn. "Their dogs are on to the scent of the Wild Boar of Ben Bulben. It's a fearsome monster that kills in an instant." Then he pointed into the darkness. "Look! There it is! We had better leave at once."

"I will not go," said Diarmuid. He didn't want to appear fainthearted in front of Fionn. "But leave Bran here to protect me."

"No," said Fionn. "The boar attacked him earlier; he's lucky to be alive."

And away he went, dragging Bran with him.

The boar was enormous. It came at Diarmuid, roaring. Diarmuid launched his spear, which did nothing but glance the boar's forehead before falling to the ground. Hooves thundering, the boar rushed at him and threw him down, ripping into him with its sharp teeth. As the blood flowed from his body, Diarmuid snatched up his sword and stabbed the boar's throat. The boar fell dead at his side. Within minutes, the Fianna arrived, Fionn Mac Cumhail with them. The warriors

were shocked to see Diarmuid lying there, injured. But Fionn Mac Cumhail smiled.

"Not so handsome now, are you, Diarmuid O'Duibhne? What woman's going to look at you now that you've lost your good looks?"

"You have the power to save my life, Fionn," said Diarmuid. "Anyone who drinks water from your hands will be cured."

Fionn did not say a word, but went to the nearby spring. Forming a cup with his hands, he lifted the water and brought it back to Diarmuid. But the water flowed through his fingers.

"You spilled the water," whispered Diarmuid.

"Why should I cure you? You stole Gráinne from me," said Fionn.

"She placed me under royal command – I had no choice. But we have all forgiven one another, have we not?"

"Never," said Fionn. And once again, he went to fetch water, and once again, the water flowed through his fingers.

The Fianna were furious to see his trickery. Oscar, Fionn's grandson, went to stand before him.

"If you don't save him I'll kill you myself!" he said.

When Fionn heard this he was afraid, because Oscar was so young and strong. He rushed away once more to fill his hands with water. But by the time he came back, Diarmuid had died …

Oscar glared at Fionn.

"Diarmuid is the best of the Fianna – our companion, our defender. You could have saved his life. And now it's too late."

Then the Fianna looked up to the sky and cried out three times. They placed their cloaks over Diarmuid's body and left him on the mountain.

When they told me that Diarmuid had died, heavy sorrow came over me. I could not speak, could only sink down and rock backwards and forwards, pulling at my hair. My screams were so loud it's said they echoed around the mountains. People ran to me to hear the terrible news.

Everyone grieved for Diarmuid, who had died on Ben Bulben. I still grieve. I will always grieve. That is the price I pay for insisting on having Diarmuid and for giving in to forgiveness. That is the price of real love. And that is why, for me, this is a story about the power of a woman.

Azenor, the Wise and Beautiful

If you should go to the city of Brest in the far west of Brittany and look out across the sea towards America, you'll see an imposing castle, standing fast between the city and the waves. The citizens of Brest call one of this castle's towers Azenor's Tower. Azenor is a melodious Breton name. But who was Azenor? This is her remarkable story …

Centuries ago, long before the city of Brest was bombed during the Second World War, longer yet before Paris claimed Brittany as part of France's territory, and certainly far and away before any French was spoken in Brittany, at the time when the Breton language was very similar to Welsh, the princess Azenor lived happily with her husband, King Alan ap Hoel Fychan, King of Brittany, in his fortified castle in Brest.

Azenor's life was busy, for she not only kept and maintained the castle but gave her husband good counsel on all his deeds as king. Some said that King Alan had much to thank Azenor for, for his success as a king was largely down to her own wisdom.

But Azenor's mother-in-law also lived in the castle – Tymyr ferch Rhun, that is, the daughter of Rhun Hir ap Maelgwn Gwynedd, which meant that she came from Wales. And, as the king's mother, Tymyr felt that no one was good enough for her precious, royal son. Alan was by now old enough to know his own mind and wore a good, thick beard but, to her, he was still her little baby – the apple of her eye.

Tymyr was aware of Azenor's influence over her husband, how, day to day, she offered wise counsel and clever ideas as to how he might better rule his kingdom and keep his people happy. Alan, in his turn, treated her with great tenderness and was obviously head over heels in love with her. All this incensed Tymyr and she would often fly into a temper, hurling priceless dishes at the castle walls, smashing them to vent her fury. One day she had an idea – a cunning way to wrest her son's attention from Azenor and claim it back herself.

Tymyr would spread lies about Azenor by whispering untruths in her son's ear, every day. Her hope was to make him lose faith and trust in his wife. From that day on, this is how it went:

"Have you seen the way she eyes up your soldiers …"

"I saw her whispering in a young man's ear …"

"There are all sorts of rumours going around in Brest, about Azenor …"

Then one day, when Alan's trust in his wife was at its lowest ebb, Tymyr came rushing over with something important to share. Out of breath from just having witnessed the alleged 'incident', Tymyr reported that she'd seen Azenor laughing and flirting with a soldier, who'd stroked her hair with blushing cheeks, obviously in love

with her. Then, according to Tymyr, the two of them disappeared into one of the castle's dark recesses and that's where Tymyr caught them, she told her son, kissing passionately in each other's arms.

On hearing this, believing every word that fell from his mother's lying lips, King Alan felt blind fury towards his wife. He called for her at once and reported his mother's accusation to her face. Azenor couldn't believe what she was hearing. But no amount protest from her made a shred of difference to her husband's opinion. He'd decided she was guilty – and that she must pay for her disrespect and for breaking her marriage vows. The soldier accused of kissing her lost his job and was thrown into jail. Azenor herself was sent forthwith to the furthest tower in the castle. There he kept her for months, and anyone walking outside, beneath the tower, would hear her crying and praying, pleading her innocence.

Now, felt Tymyr, life was much better. Now it was she who advised her son on how to rule his kingdom – just as it should be, in her own, wicked opinion. She knew very well that the whole thing was lies and trickery, and that her daughter-in-law was completely innocent, but she didn't give a fig about that, not while she had the attention and company of her precious son once more.

But Azenor's presence in the tower still made Tymyr feel uneasy. What if the passers-by beneath the tower heard her continual pleading and began to believe her? She must be got rid of, once and for all. And Tymyr knew exactly how.

"Did you know that the streets of Brest are full of rumours, my dear son?" she asked him, cunningly. "It seems that your people are calling you weak, saying that you're not a worthy king and that someone stronger should rule in your place."

"Weak? Someone else, rule in my place? Rubbish!"

"Believe me, the last thing you should do is let feelings like that spread amongst your people – if you do, they'll have you off that throne before you've so much as put your crown on in the morning. No – you must show your authority, show that no one has the right to disrespect you. You could start by executing that wicked old Azenor. Burn her alive, like a witch!"

"That sounds a little extreme, Mother … yet I don't want to lose my throne, my castle and my kingdom. I'll think about it overnight."

By morning, Alan's instinct to stay in power was stronger than ever, and so he sent orders that Azenor should be executed. She was to be burned alive before sunset that very day.

The dreaded hour arrived. A huge crowd gathered to see the terrible spectacle – for sure, everyone there was afraid of crossing Alan lest they too were burned alive. Azenor was tied to a stake that stood up from the centre of a huge mound of wood. The executioner lit a flaming torch then he set about lighting the wood beneath Azenor. But though he tried and tried, the wood refused to ignite. The flames of the torch blew, billowed and brushed the wood at Azenor's feet, but not a single piece would catch alight – as if the wood was wet with rain … though it was as dry as a bone and the cloudless evening sky glimmered with stars. It was as if Azenor was being protected by some otherworldly power.

Wild with fury and embarrassed that such a large crowd was witnessing all this, Alan ordered the executioner to prepare a barrel. Bound head and foot, Azenor was placed inside the barrel and the top was hammered down tight. At the command of King Alan, the barrel was thrown into the sea from the quay at Brest Harbour and the crowd saw it disappear between the waves. Everyone supposed that it had sunk, and that Azenor had drowned.

What they didn't realise was that the wind and the current had carried the barrel on its way across the sea. Azenor arrived in Cornwall, on the Isle of Britain, first. In Cornwall, she realised that she was going to have a baby. With faith in the barrel to carry her like a boat, she voyaged onwards in her tiny vessel, praying to reach Ireland. And so it happened. Landing safely on Ireland's shores, she settled there, working as a washerwoman for the local people, which earned her enough to bring up her son, Budok. (It is said that his name comes from the Breton word *beuzek*, which means to drown, and was given in thanks for the fact that they survived the perilous voyage.)

The years rolled by until, all of a sudden, Tymyr lay on her deathbed. King Alan sat by her side, day and night, distraught at the thought of losing his loyal mother. In her last hours, fearing that she'd go to hell for her wrongdoings, Tymyr confessed all to her son, admitting that Azenor had been completely innocent and explaining that it had been the love of a mother for her son that had led to her misdeeds. Tymyr died, leaving King Alan angry and confused. How could he have been so blind? Had Azenor really died, at her husband's hand? Remembering how they'd failed to set her alight, he couldn't help but wonder – perhaps, perhaps Azenor had managed to survive?

He set about studying maps of the sea, asking bards and counsellors of the court about wind-patterns and sea-currents at the time of Azenor's execution and for the months and years after that. At long last, he came to the conclusion that she must have gone towards the north west, possibly to Cornwall or Ireland. Without delay, he organised a ship and a crew to seek her and, to his great surprise, when he arrived in Ireland a boy was waiting for him on the shore. A boy who looked just like Alan himself. He came to learn that this was his son, and was led to Azenor. Admitting all his wrongdoings, Alan pleaded with her to return to Brittany. This she did, and Budok came to understand that he was a king's son and could have anything and everything he pleased, though he wanted for nothing. For he'd known since his birth that he had a very special mother. A mother who'd given her name to a part of Brest Castle that is called to this day Azenor's Tower.

Pennard Castle

If you go to the Gower Peninsula today and wander along its shores, you'll come across the ruins of an old castle, crouching in the sand. This is Pennard Castle, drowned by sand dunes. But why, you wonder, has it been abandoned like this, and for so many centuries? Well, the story begins at the other end of Wales in Gwynedd, in a garden in the small hours of the morning.

Princess Angharad was lying on her back in the garden, eyes closed. She wasn't sleeping. She was listening. Not to the commotion at the palace or the horses whinnying as someone tightened their saddles, or to the laughter of the unfamiliar soldiers with their strange accents. She was listening for the whir of tiny wings, beating in the air by her ear. She was listening for the patter of little feet, landing in dew. She was listening for voices quieter than a whisper, telling her that everything would be all right. She was listening to hear the *Tylwyth Teg* – the Fair Folk.

Angharad knew they were there – she'd seen them before. One of them had touched her, when she was a little girl. She'd slipped and fallen on stones, grazing her legs, and was lying on the ground and crying. A she-fairy had come to her and gently laid her hand on Angharad's knee.

Instantly, Angharad had felt better. But by the time she'd dried her tears and turned to thank the little fairy, she'd disappeared once more into the leaves.

Angharad found tears welling in her eyes again that morning. She had made so many memories in this castle, her home, but today she was to say farewell to them all. Her father, the King of Gwynedd, had sworn an oath to Lord Pennard that Angharad would go to him to be his wife, if he would agree to support the King of Gwynedd in battle. The lord had consented to this, sending his own soldiers to fight with the king. And so it appeared that Angharad was marrying him as part of the bargain. But in truth she was going there as a spy, to keep an eye on this disreputable lord – because the King of Gwynedd didn't trust him at all.

One small tear ran down the side of her cheek when she thought of the long journey that awaited her. But as she felt more tears pooling in her eyes and the sob rising in her throat, she heard a sound. A tiny wee sound … like a little mouse, sneezing by her ear. She opened her eyes and turned her head towards it, and there stood a sopping-wet she-fairy. Angharad's tear had landed on her head and given her a drenching. But before Angharad could say a word, the fairy disappeared amongst the flowers. At that, a shout came from the castle. Lord Pennard's horses and his soldiers were ready to leave for the land of the Gower.

The Gower was a long way from Gwynedd and it took them days to travel there. The weather was miserable and damp seeped into Angharad's clothes, making her cold. The soldiers escorting her didn't have much to say to her. She felt lonely, so very lonely. At least she could look forward to her welcome at the castle, she thought, to hot food in her belly and a good fire to warm her. But she was to be disappointed. There wasn't much of a welcome for the princess – or for the soldiers, to tell the truth – when at last they arrived at Pennard Castle. By this time, she was exhausted and longed to warm herself before the fire. But the lord didn't have much sympathy.

"I wish to keep all the food for our wedding feast. Dry bread will do for you until then … and don't think I'm wasting firewood on you either." As he spat these cold words he scarfed down a piece of meat, right in front of her.

He was a selfish man, and there was not a grain of kindness in him. That night, Angharad went to bed starving and cold – as she did every night that followed, to tell the truth. She soon began to feel low and miserable. This was not a happy home for her.

At night, when she couldn't sleep, she'd listen intently. She was certain she could hear tiny peals of laughter and the sound of little creatures hurrying between the flowers outside. I wonder … she thought … I wonder if the Fair Folk have followed me? But every time she went to the window to try to see them in the moon's light, there was nothing there. No, she must have been dreaming.

When the day of the wedding feast came, Lord Pennard was even more irritable than ever – bellowing at his servants, who were trying their best to prepare for the party on empty stomachs. He wanted everything to be perfect and magnificently grand, to impress his important guests. But as the day went on, things started to go awry. At first it was the disappearing apples.

"Which little devils are stealing the apples?" screeched the lord, mad as a wasp.

Then the wine began to sour.

"Yuuuck! What rogue has soured the wine?" snarled the lord, viciously.

Afraid for their lives, the man-servants and the maids all swore blind they weren't behind this mischief.

Then the lord heard tiny, giggling voices from the garden. He peered through the window but he couldn't see a thing.

"Children …" he growled. "I hate naughty children! Go and get rid of them," he yelled to his servants, who ran straight out into the garden.

Angharad kept quiet. She had a better idea who it was that was causing trouble for this disagreeable lord.

The servants came back in a hurry, full of wonder.

"My Lord ... they aren't children ... but the *Tylwyth Teg* – the Fair Folk!"

"The Fair Folk?" The lord spat the words. He hated the Fair Folk. That lot are even worse than children, he thought. "Gather them up and throw them out of here ... there's no welcome for the *Tylwyth Teg* at Pennard Castle."

When Angharad heard this, she got to her feet. The castle began to shake as a mighty wind rose with her, swirling about the princess.

"You had better listen, Lord Pennard ..." said Angharad, her words strong and sure over the roar of the wind.

"Huh ... listen to you? Don't talk rot!" he raged, in his arrogance.

"No, not to me," said Angharad, firmly. "Listen to the wind ..."

Then everyone heard the little voices on the wind, singing:

"Be you careful, do you no
Harm to us, the fairy folk;
Be you careful, revenge is nigh
Revenge, revenge is at hand nearby."

Lord Pennard burst into laughter. He strode menacingly towards Angharad and thrust his face into hers until she could smell his stinking breath.

"I'm not afraid of the Fair Folk." He turned to bellow at his servants once more. "Get out, underlings, and drive them away. There's no place for the likes of them in Pennard Castle."

At that moment, Angharad knew that she could no longer stand to be in Pennard Castle – no longer stand to be anywhere near this hideous lord for another moment. She turned on her heel and strode out of the room.

By then, the wind was roaring so deafeningly that Angharad couldn't hear Lord Pennard shouting after her and screaming at the servants to get rid of the Fair Folk. The wind was so strong it was lifting huge drifts of sand and driving them mercilessly against the castle walls.

Angharad pressed her heels into her horse's flanks and galloped away from Pennard Castle, leaving the sand storm to overwhelm its stone walls. She reached a small hill and halted to look back at the castle for one last time. She knew that the power of the *Tylwyth Teg*, the Fair Folk, had caused this mighty storm above Pennard Castle in the land of the Gower. She tugged at the horse's mane and they raced from there at speed. Neither she, nor anyone else, ever saw the Lord of Pennard Castle again.

And that's the story of the castle that drowns under sand on the Gower Peninsular. Amazing to think that such tiny things can do so much damage, isn't it?

Cailleach – Keeper of the Deer

"Brrr!" The wind has turned and it's slicing down from the far north like a knife blade. There, the old woman called Cailleach is waking from the long, deep sleep that carried her through the months of summer. It's the Feast of Samhain – All Hallow's Eve – and the dark evenings are here again. Prepare yourself, because Cailleach is about to spread her magic over the Highlands of Scotland and beyond. She has many names – Queen of the Hoarfrost, Winter's Hag. Her pure white hair has been washed in the freezing whirlpool of Corryvreckan until little pearls of ice cling to its locks. She will flit across the ground, but if you should meet her, beware – one glimpse of her face is enough to freeze you with fear. Her skin is blue-grey, her teeth are blood-red, and her single eye can see into the depths of your heart … and from this world into the next.

In her hand she carries a stout staff and, as she wanders about, she will strike at the earth to freeze the land and the lochs, until everywhere is turned to icy desert. But despite her terrifying appearance, Cailleach isn't all bad. Though she's Winter's Hag, intent on turning the

ground to frost and snow, she also watches carefully over her land. She is Keeper of the Highland Deer, and she looks after them as devotedly as if they were her own children.

And now you know something about Cailleach. You'll find legends about her everywhere in Scotland; legends of how, by casting huge rocks here and there or striking the ground with her staff, she created the mountains and valleys, the lochs, rivers and glens that cover the country. But no one knows everything about Cailleach, for so much magic swirls around her.

Once, Cailleach awoke from her deep sleep, ready for the work of spreading white frost over the land of the Scots, when she noticed a nobleman wandering through a wood, a bow in his hand. This, so they said, was an important man of these parts, and it was his intention to hold a feast in his castle. He would invite his noble companions to join in the feast, and of course he would need venison – deer meat – to eat, and an excess of everything.

Now, Cailleach allowed hunters to take deer, on occasion – but only if they asked her permission first. And, of course, they must not shoot at random – after all, one deer would give plenty enough venison for a feast. Keeping the deer was a serious responsibility, for the deer played an important role in the landscape and wildlife of Scotland. And though Cailleach was a frightening goddess to many, others saw her as a wise and careful one. It was she who kept the seeds safe underground

until the time came for them to wake in the spring. It was she who made sure that small creatures could hibernate comfortably. It was she, too, that woke them when it was time for her to depart the land. And it was Cailleach who watched over the deer in winter, leaving parts of the glens clear of snow so that they might find sustenance by grazing there.

Not far from the nobleman's castle there lived a poor man in a little cottage. He was an old, old man, old enough to know the habits and hexes of the Winter's Hag.

"Remember to ask permission from Cailleach before you go a-hunting today," said the old man when he saw the nobleman and his men preparing to set out.

"Huh!" dismissed the nobleman. "I don't need to ask anyone's permission to shoot my own deer. I hunt within my castle's grounds so, if there are deer in these woods they're *my* deer and I have the right to kill as many as I please."

"Well, you do that and you're certain-sure to provoke Cailleach's ire," noted the old man. He knew Cailleach's temperament very well; he knew how she gave with one hand and took with the other. The old man nodded wisely and went back to his house, where he packed his possessions into a little sack. He was going to go and stay with his daughter in the next valley, just in case.

The nobleman and his hunters galloped towards the woods where the deer were sheltering. There was a herd of them – young deer and old deer, a few grey hinds and, at their head, the great, antlered stag, his coat as red as autumn bracken. This winter Cailleach had worried terribly about Scotland's wildlife – so many small creatures had disappeared from the land as their habitats were destroyed by people. This made her even more determined to defend her deer.

The hunters crept on horseback around the trunks of trees, their eyes peeled, their arrows at the ready ... then, suddenly, a young hind leapt from cover and out on to open ground. The rest of the herd sensed danger but, instead of staying still and hiding, they followed the hind. Off they all sprang, leaping across streams, jumping over stones and rocks and up on to the sides of the valley, where there was nothing but heather and bracken – nothing to shelter them, no trees to hide behind. The stag galloped in front, his antlers high and graceful in the cold air, and the herd followed at a sprint across the slopes as the hooves of the hunters' horses closed on them with every second. The nobleman's horse climbed up above the glen and from there he could aim down at the deer. He waited there on the slope and, with his bow, aimed an arrow at a young hind – "Sshsshssh ..." The arrow flew and hit the hind in the side of her throat. She fell to the ground, still.

The hind would have been enough meat for the feast, but the nobleman wanted to claim the stag, too. As the rest of the herd disappeared over the ridge, the stag halted for a minute, his magnificent head looking back across the glen, his eyes full of sadness. "Sshsshsshsshssh ..." The arrow flew and hit him. He slipped to the ground, dead.

The hunter gave a shout of triumph. Not one but two deer shot – there'd be a feast and a half tonight! And to crown it all, he had the head of the stag as a prize, to be proudly displayed on the wall of his castle.

But Cailleach was close by. She'd heard the hissing of the arrows, and she'd rushed to lead the rest of the herd away to safety, her pure white hair spreading thick, cold mist across the valley floor behind her. She ran and ran, until she'd taken the deer far from the land of the nobleman and his arrows.

Now, it was Cailleach's custom to look after a spring on top of a mountain called Ben Cruachan. Every night, she made sure to replace the lid of the spring – a very responsible job because, if the lid was left off, the spring's water would not stop flowing down the mountain ... Here in Wales we know all about what happens when a flow of water isn't stopped. Remember Seithennyn and the doors of Cantre'r Gwaelod – the city that drowned beneath the sea? Well, Cailleach had worked hard all day and was tired out. She managed to climb to the summit of Ben Cruachan that night, but she was so exhausted that, instead of putting the lid straight back on the spring after taking a drink of water, she decided to sit down for a minute. Only a minute. But then she fell asleep! Cailleach slept heavily, while water flowed down the slopes of the mountain and collected in the glen below. The water flowed all through the night before Cailleach jolted awake and looked down at where the glen had been. There before her was a wide loch.

No one knows for certain what happened to the nobleman and his friends. But you can be sure there was plenty of venison for them to eat at the feast, and certainly there was plenty of wine and beer to drink too. There would have been much celebration, because shooting a mighty and dignified stag was thought of as quite a feat.

Everyone would have congratulated the gentleman and looked admiringly at the stag's head, hanging on the wall of his castle. And, surely, everyone would have been so busy carousing that no one would have noticed the little stream outside that swelled until it overflowed its banks. No one would have seen the water rising, bit by bit, around the castle and the woods, as it flowed down to cover the floor of the glen, until all that was left was a shining layer of freezing water. And when the wise old man came back after visiting his daughter in the next valley, he laughed sadly and looked up to the sky. There he caught a glimpse of someone flying past, her pure white hair spreading thick mist across the flooded glen.

No one is sure any longer where this glen is – but perhaps Loch Awe is the lake? No one is sure, either, if there is a castle there, under the water. But deer still wander in Scotland's glens. No one is sure who looks after them, but they always seem to know how to find food, though the ground is often frozen solid. And every year the seasons turn and winter's hoarfrost retreats, allowing the little animals of spring to awaken again.

Queen Lupa of Galicia

Pen Draw'r Byd is a place name that means World's End in Welsh. And there's a Pen Draw'r Byd – a World's End – to be found in many other Celtic lands, too. As well as sharing the same name, they're all places that look similar. They all have rugged cliffs, wild seas, huge boulders and exposed rocks. And one or two little sandy bays between headlands, with only just enough room for a small ship to come ashore. The early Celts, so they say, reached the land from the sea.

Imagine a little ship with a single mast and sail, departing the Scottish Isles some thousand years ago. She's sailing south and meeting storms that blow westwards towards her from the Irish Sea. Most Celtic lands face these western winds. The ship, with her small crew of sailors, is voyaging past Ireland's cliffs. Over there is the Isle of Man, rising from the waves one morning and, on the horizon by the afternoon, here comes the long row of Cymru's mountains. Onwards, then, past the islands and mainlands of Cornwall and Brittany, the sea churned white at the foot of their rocks.

There's a long, wide bay to cross after that then, one morning, wild, rugged cliffs hove into view once more.

"Where are we now?" The question came from the youngest of the crew. He was making this voyage for the first time.

"See that arm of land over there? That's Pen Draw'r Byd – the World's End," one of the experienced sailors told him. "And the high mountains there, that tower up on the horizon behind it? Those were Queen Lupa's lands."

"And what sort of a person was she?"

"Oh! She was surely strong, brave, determined – and a bit of a she-fox and right wild with it too – for to keep order on the men of that land. Galicia is the name of the country."

"Was she really like that, was she?"

"Who now?"

"Queen Lupa. Was she really a little bit wild and an old she-fox and …?"

"Spells in shells! Was she ever! There are many stories told about her, though she be dead now for a thousand years …"

"And can we understand the language of these Galicians – the language of the stories?"

"Oh, we can, to be sure. Galego is the name of their language, and though they live beside the people of Spain and the Basques and the Portuguese, they are Celts to their core. Celts, just like us. Only Celts can live on sea and rocks such as these."

"What about her, then?"

"What then?"

"Well, am I going to hear one of these stories, about Queen Lupa of Galicia?"

"Let's pass the World's End first. We want to head for that bay there at the foot of the mountains. There lies the small, sheltered harbour of Padrón. There, we can leave the ship for a while.

And I'll take you up to the church in the town of Padrón to see the most wondrous ship that ever sailed the crest of a wave. A ship made of stone, she is …"

"A ship made of stone? She never is!"

"Just you wait till we get to the church at Padrón, my boy."

By the quay at Padrón, two shell-fishers helped the sailors guide their ship into shore and secure her. Then they directed one of the crew to a spring, where he might fill the ship's flasks with fresh drinking water. Another of the seamen went to find bread and a little food.

"We've plenty of time," said the old mariner to the lad. "Let's go to the church."

"Here she is!" said the youth, when he saw the large stone altar in the church of Santiago de Padrón – Saint James of Padrón. "You told me that Herod beheaded James the Apostle in the land of Canaan and then some of the other disciples took the body all the way across the Middle Sea on this stone! And that it floated over the surface of the water!"

"An angel pushed it, so they say," said the storyteller, without turning a hair. "The purpose of the voyage was to bury Saint James in the land where he best loved to preach about Christ – namely, Galicia. Queen Lupa – you know, the woman from the mountain – owned the land where this marvellous cargo came ashore, but she wasn't about to give up a finger's-width of her ground to bury an apostle. Like I said, she was an old she-fox."

"What did she do, then?"

"'Go and see the governor of this land,' she told the disciples. 'He is a Roman of the very best kind.' But in truth he was one of the cruellest proconsuls of the Roman

Empire. No sooner had the disciples come before him than he had them thrown into the dungeon of his prison. But, as luck would have it, the angel was still around and, by some miracle or another, the disciples managed to escape. The Romans went after them. And, as the disciples were pursued over the bridge of the Rio Tambre, it collapsed behind them into the river's torrent, drowning every single Roman."

"Did the disciples go back to seek revenge on Queen Lupa?"

"Lupa was full of apologies. It'd all been a misunderstanding, she said. But to make up for their ill treatment she had a present for them, she went on. She would give them two oxen and a cart so they might carry the body to its special burial place. All they need do was fetch these oxen from the mountain of Monte Ilicino – and then the two oxen would help them build a beautiful burial tomb for James the Apostle."

"Was it another trick?"

"It surely was. There was a dangerous dragon on the top of Monte Ilicino and, what's more, they found there not two placid oxen but two raging bulls! But the angel appeared once more, to save their skins. And before you knew it the bulls had been turned into biddable beasts, who couldn't do enough to help the cause. It was they, according to the story, that chose the burial place in the end, deep within a cave in the mountains. For centuries, no one knew its whereabouts. But then, some hundred years ago, the body was moved to a church where a large tomb was built for it in a town that was renamed Santiago de Compostela. Ever since then, pilgrims walk hundreds of miles along what is called the Way of Saint James, for to visit the grave. And, of course, lots of Celts travel there too, from over the sea. This voyage is an easy one for us, as you know."

"Surely the thousands of pilgrims have been good for Santiago's businesses?" said the lad. "Strange that Queen Lupa didn't think of that!"

"Lupa had no interest in saints or pilgrims. Held on to the old beliefs, she did," said the old mariner. "But you're right, of course. By now, Santiago is the third most important city in the Christian world. The place is well worth seeing. There are plenty of rocks in Galicia, as you saw on the voyage. But there are plenty of craftsmen here too, to carve shapeless boulders into beautiful buildings. And to make statues and effigies of gold and precious ores. You see, though the lands of the World's End may look wild and bare, there are great riches to be found within its rocks. But here we are – it's time for us to turn to our own business now. I must go to meet with the merchants, as I've come to collect the barrels of wine and the casket of gold we crossed the sea for. Off you go back to ship to help unload the casks of iron ore."

The ship was on the beach at Padrón for three nights.

It was heavy work, unloading and loading cargo. The bargaining between the sailors and the Galician merchants was hard work too. But, by the final night, everyone was satisfied and everyone was friends.

The shell-fishers brought sacks full of shellfish and opened them on the beach in front of the inn. Some of the boys from town arrived with bundles of firewood and the wooden staves of smashed up old barrels, and before long a fine fire was blazing on the beach. A piper and a harpist turned up from somewhere and the innkeeper came out carrying a huge pitcher of wine for them to share. No, put your money away, he announced – the wine merchant has paid for it all.

The gold merchant had brought his family with him to sit around the fire while the fishermen cooked their shellfish on the flames and shared their delicacies with the Celts from the northern lands. This seafood was presented to everyone at the fireside feast by placing a single shell into each hand.

"Goodness me, but these are delicious!" said the youth. "What are they?"

"There are all kinds of wholesome foods to be had from the seas that surround the Celtic lands, as you know," began the old mariner. "At home we eat fish, of course, but also seaweed, mussels, winkles and cockles. But, here, surely, we have the king of all shellfish. It's called a scallop. Look at the shape of the shell in your hand. Turn it over. You see a picture like the sun setting? Or the sun rising, perhaps? See how the ridges of the shell look like sunbeams, that come together at the bottom in a powerful, welcoming place. This is the pilgrims' shell. They look for this shell as they walk along these shores on their journeys to Santiago de Compostela, for the shells' beams are the paths that come from many directions to meet in that sacred city. The pilgrims leave shells in trees, on rocks and by the side of the path to show the way to the pilgrims that follow them. They wear them in their hats and on their clothes, and tie them to the tops of their walking sticks, to indicate that they're pilgrims. They use the shells to collect water from springs and founts on the journey. And, of course, they search for them along the shores to eat them! Yes indeed, they're maddeningly tasty! Santiago's shells – that's what they call them in these lands."

One of the gold merchant's daughters stood up to sing a magical song, full of *hiraeth* – that is, longing and sadness – and the harmonies of the sea's waves. The young man was reminded of his home in the village by the north Celtic sea and realised how alike this song was to one they sang there. As the bagpipe and the harp joined the melody, he thought of the sea-paths that lay ahead of them, the very next day. And he hoped that the spirit of Saint James – not the ghost of Queen Lupa – would lead them over the waves and safely home.

About the Stories

Golden-headed Niamh

An Irish legend, retold by Angharad Tomos

There are many Celtic stories about the land (or island) called Tir na-nÓg, where people remain forever young. This is one of them.

Rhiannon and the Punishment of Being a Horse

A Welsh legend, retold by Myrddin ap Dafydd

The legend of Rhiannon is one of a collection of old Welsh myths called *The Mabinogi*. The four 'branches' of *The Mabinogi* tell us Pryderi's life story – a character who plays an important role in this tale about Rhiannon.

Ker Is

A Breton legend, retold by Aneirin Karadog

All along the Celtic coasts, and by one or two lakes as well, legends like this are told about the power of water that rises to drown valuable lands.

Morag the Clever

A Scottish legend, retold by Mari George

Women with ancient wisdom and knowledge, granting them powers beyond their natural strength, are a common theme in Celtic storytelling. And so is fooling the fairies and their magic tricks!

The Giants of Karrek Loos yn Koos

A Cornish legend, retold by Branwen Williams

In south-west Cornwall there's a rocky island topped by a castle called St Michael's Mount. The Celts are fond of explaining mounds of rocks with legends about giants – and this is a good example.

The Mermaid of Purt le Moirrey

A legend from the Isle of Man, retold by Anni Llŷn

Mermaids are often found in Celtic legends. These magical, dangerous beings must be treated very carefully, as we learn in this story.

An Eye for an Eye

An Irish legend, retold by Haf Llewelyn

There are many untamed, headstrong princesses in Celtic tales, and some of them are drunk with power. There are also stories about wrongdoing, leading to revenge – and both these themes appear in this legend.

Rhos y Pawl

A Welsh legend, retold by Angharad Tomos

Pure love, love that overcomes all, is at the very centre of this legend from the heart of the mountains of Eryri in North Wales.

The Daughter of the Waves

A Scottish legend, retold by Myrddin ap Dafydd

Seals are found all along the coasts of Celtic lands. A seal's skeleton is remarkably similar to a human's – but without arms and legs. 'The children of the sea' is the name given to seals in many Celtic languages, and legends like this one weave us humans together with these beautiful sea creatures.

The Adventure of Keresen of Sen Senar

A Cornish legend, retold by Branwen Williams

The ability of humankind to see the fair folk, or the little people – often with the help of a special ointment – is something that all fairies abhor. Here is one of the Celtic legends that outlines this.

The Story of Gráinne

An Irish legend, retold by Mari George

The essence of this story is the jealousy of a husband towards his wife. It's about what happens when a man treats a woman as if she is one of his belongings.

Azenor, the Wise and Beautiful

A Breton legend, retold by Aneirin Karadog

A common theme in Celtic legends is that of a poisonous mother who hates her son's wife. And there couldn't be a more extreme example than the mother in this story!

Pennard Castle

A Welsh legend, retold by Anni Llŷn

Pennard Castle was built on the Gower by the Normans, and this legend gives us a flavour of the conflict between the Welsh and these tyrants. But this time the *Tylwyth Teg*, or the Fair People, come along to right the wrongs inflicted on the gentle and the good.

Cailleach – Keeper of the Deer

A Scottish legend, retold by Haf Llewelyn

Winter is portrayed as a hag, or a witch, in this story – but she's also a witch who acts as a guardian for wildlife. Closeness to nature, and living in harmony with it, is found everywhere in the Celtic world.

Queen Lupa of Galicia

A Galician legend, retold by Myrddin ap Dafydd

In a little corner of Europe, just above Portugal, lies the Celtic land of Galicia. Some three million people live there nowadays, and sixty-five per cent of them speak their own language, called Galego. This is another story about seafarers and a powerful queen.